Stories from the Cent

Stories from the Center

Connecting Narrative and Theory
in the Writing Center

Edited by

Lynn Craigue Briggs
Eastern Washington University

Meg Woolbright
Siena College

National Council of Teachers of English
1111 W. Kenyon Road, Urbana, Illinois 61801-1096

Prepress: City Desktop Productions, Inc.
Production Editor: Rita D. Disroe
Interior Design: Tom Kovacs for TGK Design
Cover Design: City Desktop Productions, Inc.

NCTE Stock Number: 47461-3050

Library of Congress Cataloging-in-Publication Data

Stories from the center : connecting narrative and theory in the writing center /
[edited] by Lynn Craigue Briggs, Meg Woolbright.
     p.   cm.
   Includes bibliographical references and index.
   ISBN 0-8141-4746-1
   1. English language—Rhetoric—Study and teaching. 2. Report writing—
Study and teaching. 3. English teachers—Attitudes. 4. Teacher-student
relationships. 5. Writing centers. I. Briggs, Lynn Craigue, 1960– II.
Woolbright, Meg, 1955–

PE1404.S834 1999
808'.042'07—dc21   99-052503

This book was typeset in Palatino by City Desktop Productions, Inc.

Typefaces used on the cover were Benguiat and Palatino.

The book was printed on 60-lb. Lynx Opaque by Versa Press.

Contents

Acknowledgments

We would like to thank our patient, creative, hardworking contributors. We would also like to thank the Larrys—Woolbright and Briggs—for their unfailing support. And Nick Briggs for asking, "Mom, are you done editing that book yet?" Of course, none of this would have been possible without the nimble fingers and careful eyes of Ellen Johnson. The pets Rex, Cora, Rock, Beenie, and Emily helped to keep things in perspective by reminding us that there are forms of life on this planet who prosper without even conceptualizing academia and scholarship.

Introduction: Reflections on Editing

Lynn Craigue Briggs
Eastern Washington University

Meg Woolbright
Siena College

"We are healed by our stories."

—Terry Tempest Williams

Background

Our eyes met in the mirror across the crowded Boston restroom. "Meg?" "Lynn?" we asked. It was a CCCC's renewal of a conference friendship, a renewal that precipitated phone calls in which we told stories and hatched the idea for this book.

Between the two of us, we've spent over a quarter century in writing centers. During this time, we've both marveled at the richness of writing center conversations and have been disappointed because so little of this richness has made its way into publicly authorized forms.

This book resulted from our desires, desires that had rarely been fulfilled by what was available in print about writing centers. As writing center directors, we often had the opportunity to hear stories, but rarely had the opportunity to reflect upon their meanings. The stories people told us, in our roles as directors, were usually told for an immediate purpose—to convince us to solve a problem. In between solving our centers' problems, we sometimes wondered what lessons could be learned from these stories. Sometimes when we talked to each other we puzzled and wondered about the stories we had heard. We brought the stories that haunted or inspired us out into the open. We found it useful to discuss with each other the stories our center staff told us. And we thought, "Wouldn't it be nice to extend this, to make the stories available without the long-distance phone bills?"

Some of these long-distance calls were spent puzzling over the fact that so many publications about writing centers seemed to sweep away complexity, to reduce tutoring/consulting/responding to a set of seven steps or five categories, to streamline policy and procedures, and to offer simple "solutions" to "problems." We saw an opportunity to resist this construction with a collection of rich narratives, stories from the center, in which authors wrote about lived experiences and reflected on those experiences in terms of current theory.

This is the book we wanted to read, and therefore, the book we have edited.

A Little Rationale(ity)

We were not the only folks in the field sharing stories. There was much writing center talk taking place in a variety of settings: at professional conferences, over lunch, in hallways, over WCenter (the e-mail network). In our conversations, writing centers became microcosms of pedagogical, textual, and human relations, not on the periphery but at the center of language, literacy, and learning. At this center, things converge. In this convergence, we come into direct and immediate contact with a multitude of sometimes conflicting strands: with students—such as Li, who doesn't look up from his grammar workbook until his last session with writing coach Stephen Jukuri, when he suddenly displays pictures of "home," then disappears; with colleagues such as Patty Dunn's, who challenge her philosophy and authority with their comments on students' texts. In this "center," we come face to face not only with the multiple subjectivities of real people, but with complex theories of how their positions are constructed and maintained. Theories of language, literacy, and learning are played out in our daily interactions.

More often than not, these writing center conversations are stories, stories repeated and mused over, stories that stay with us—for whatever reason. These stories constitute our professional knowledge; they need to be trusted; they need to be taken seriously. They need to be shared publicly.

It seemed simple and straightforward—a collection of stories about the writing center in which contributors puzzled about their stories, and connected the stories to theory that they found important. It seemed odd, on reflection, that no one had done this before.

But when we started to tell the story of wanting to do this volume, we found that its simplicity seemed to make it a challenge. The notion of narrative for academic purposes wasn't so commonsensical.

Story vs. Study

One of the things we learned from those who generously sent drafts to us was that the socialization process in academe was moving away from narrative and toward exposition and this movement was strong. We received many interesting and valuable studies from hopeful contributors, studies that intrigued and informed us; however, these were studies and not stories, and therefore, did not fit with what we had in mind.

This led us to consider the distinction between a "study" and a "story." A study, it seems to us, is a story of sorts, but a story about other people's lives, with others' voices and others' authorities dominating. A story has a point of contact with one's own life. A study makes some attempt or pretense at being controlled or objective, whereas, a story considers events in light of their own subjectivity. We think that scholars have been taught to devalue their own stories; we wanted to compile this volume, in part, to ask our readers to reevaluate that lesson.

In the chapters that follow, our contributors not only tell us the subjective tales of their writing center lives, but reflect on how their subjectivities were formed, they try to figure out what forces shaped their perceptions, and, whenever possible, they connect the stories to theories they have thought through.

We wanted actively to resist what we call "study" discourse—the distanced, measured telling of events. We wanted to resist it not only to be resistant, but also to put pressure on the discourse of our field, to question implicitly the notion that we must use study-like language to gain respect. We think that such resistance will strengthen the field as we all begin to question our discursive assumptions and decisions.

We believe that story can offer an entree into our undergraduate and graduate students' lives and send them a message that the language that we use to construct our own lives is valued and valuable for teaching.

We also hope to advance the cause of narrative in academe, because we believe that we need a variety of discourse forms to capture the array of important thoughts in the field. Narrative provides a way to speak things otherwise unspeakable, to give voice to that which would otherwise go unheard.

After six years we would also like to assert that writing (and editing) narrative is as rigorous as writing non-narrative discourse. We wonder if narrative has been devalued because it is the discourse of fairy tales, dinner conversation, pillow talk. While we want to value those storytelling situations, we also want to draw distinctions between these forms of narrative and the academic narratives included in this volume. What we offer here are two specific types of narratives—forms that we wish to call academic narrative—that tangle story and theory inextricably.

We hope that this volume can help folks in our field reclaim their stories, to relearn to trust their narrative selves, and to dwell on the stories that haunt or inspire them.

Intertwining Story and Theory

Our contributors demonstrate two different ways that story can be intertwined with theory as an academic discourse form. One group uses theory as a way to read the story, the other uses story as a way to read the theory. Sometimes story is the lens that brings theory into clearer focus; sometimes theory clarifies story.

Those contributors who use theory as a lens through which to read story also use theory as a way to make sense, knit together, or even dispossess a story of its haunting power. These contributors seem to take comfort in theory—the presence of another's theory seems to suggest that they are not alone, that their stories, although unique, are not aberrations. Most of the contributors who use theory to make sense of story—Mark Hurlbert, Michael Blitz, Joe Janangelo, and Jan Wolff—relate stories of restlessness in relationships. They seem to use theory to make some sort of peace with stories of these relationships. They use theory to help themselves slow the stories down and reflect their way to new positions on the relationships.

The level of abstraction characteristic of theory enables it to be applied to many different sets of experience. Patty Dunn, Beth Boquet, Laura Rogers, Carolyn Statler, Stephen Jukuri, Lynn Briggs and Kate Latterell all apply theory to their stories. As a result, the theory is illuminated. The stories provide particular handles for theory, handles that enable these writers to stretch and test theory. These stories show how theory works and how the intricacies of writing center interaction demonstrate aspects of theory. Like theory, these stories, although vivid and specific, become generalizable, as testaments to how theory works. These contributors write about larger issues—professional roles, institutional constraints and the multiplicity of subject positions for writing center personnel.

Foreshadowing

Lynn Briggs's chapter tells the story of her long-term writing center relationship with Mary Ann to illustrate Cooper's "web of readers," and to speculate on how academic culture forces coherence on writers. By examining the web of readers that she and Mary Ann make visible in their writing center sessions, Lynn considers how troubling the academic construct of "coherence" can be. She also speculates on how emergent technologies metaphorically challenge that construct.

While Lynn explicitly challenges the need for coherence, Beth Boquet's quilted recollections do so implicitly. Beth explores the pieces of the writing center system—training, interaction with students, paperwork—and how those pieces are managed by the center staff to paint a particular portrait of the institution. She uses Goffman's metaphor of the world as a stage, and all the participants in the writing center ecology are "stepping into a role that already exists," where little "improvisation is allowed." In Beth's story another tutor, Shelly, attempts to take control over her role, to improvise, as it were, by not filling out the paperwork. Shelly's petulant resistance is ironically juxtaposed with real reasons for resistance—the way that documents and documentation seek and serve to control workers, and to make people complicit in institutional schemes.

Beth tells of working with Tom, a writer whose institutional roles have been blurred. He is a recent veteran and a returning student. His interpretations of his place in the system conflict with Beth's. She is annoyed with Tom for his militaristic ideology, and yet when she reflects upon her own views she sees that as a tutor, she is also someone who has "mastered the discourse and internalized the ideology of the institution."

While the issues of gender and power echo throughout the center in Beth's story, Patty Dunn's tale reminds us that the center is located in a politicized institution. Patty worries that writing for this collection is the cowardly way out of a dialogue she should have with a senior colleague (one with a vote on her tenure) about her being "soft" on grammar. As a writing center director, Patty considers the ecological system of response and how one's position in this hierarchical system affects the kind of response one can provide. She connects rhetorical constructs to this hierarchy, and considers how concepts like the "thesis" end up writing the student. She tells of Tara, a writer who is disabled as a reader because of her writing instruction, which taught her that good writing presents a clear thesis. Patty laments the fact that in the academic system, having something for faculty to profess—for example, strict rules about grammar—sometimes prevents teachers from teaching the kind of analytic reflection that universities ostensibly exist to promote.

As Patty feels at risk because of her philosophy at the center, Jan Wolff challenges herself to make the center's contact zone a safe house for at-risk students. Jan uses Pratt's notion of a "contact zone" to describe her work with Trevor. Somehow she and Trevor are able to negotiate a safe house within the power imbalances of the contact zone, where Trevor occasionally experiences incomprehension, but "never the rage" Pratt associates with the zone.

This is a story of reciprocal learning—while only the knowledge from Jan's side is privileged, the information and insights from Trevor's side are valued in the center. In fact, contact with Trevor enables Jan to reevaluate her specialist stance and language. Jan realizes that Trevor's contribution to her knowledge of the world goes beyond translation of gang symbols and right to the heart of her expertise.

The contact zone in which Jan operates provides a place for alien cultures to interface. Stephen Jukuri teases out his multiple writing center subjectivities and examines the way they interface (or fail to). Stephen explores his and his writers' multiple subjectivities in the center; he ponders what it might be to follow Holzman's advice to "replace relationships within roles" with relationships between individuals. Stephen tells the tale of his interactions with Carla, Li, Russ, Dan, and Jim and demonstrates how many different subject positions he takes, and pushes others into, in the center. He also paints a picture of lives that are tangled together, of writing center relationships that won't remain only writing center relationships, of subject positions that won't remain fixed.

Stephen's examination of his multiple subjectivities illuminates how many voices can be ventriloquated through one writing center coach. Laura Rogers and Carolyn Statler examine this multivocality within the challenging parameters of a writing center in which tutors literally are supposed to speak for teachers. Laura and Carolyn tell of working in their writing center, which has the practice of de- and recontextualizing student writing. At this center, writing center instructors are the primary readers of papers written for other classes. Laura and Carolyn use the work of Bakhtin and Knoblauch to understand their work with writers Mary, Jim, Linda, and Jane in the material context in which their writing center is situated. They consider the way that their institution had cast these writers as "rogues" or "clowns," and how working with writing center instructors was supposed to norm or "center" these kinds of writers. They share their regrets over how the system caused them to distrust their reactions to Mary, made them go through channels, and, in essence, be less able to help Mary do what Knoblauch encourages us to do—work "toward the improvement of [her] condition."

While Carolyn and Laura consider the dialogic nature of writing center work, Mark Hurlbert and Michael Blitz write a chapter born of e-mail dialogues that are much like the give-and-take of center response sessions. Their chapter demonstrates the synergy of collaboration as they consider some of the complex political issues which are often seen in discussions of composition, but often absent from writing center talk. Mark and Michael use the stories of Gloria and Anthony, of Erika and Leana, to remind us that ESL students in the writing center aren't just bringing with them different vocabularies and syntax, but different possibilities and fears. Gloria wanted Mark to "fix" her English. After Gloria disappeared, her ghost has made it harder and more urgent for Mark to get a "fix" on who and what are important in the academy.

In Michael and Mark's story, tutors Erika and Leana discovered that one person's periphery is another's center. Through an exploration of language, Erika, Leana, and writer Sonya also explored social class. In a collaboration full of laughter, they created a safe place for one another in the center—a place where—for the moment, getting "fixed," "a fix," or academic fixations had no place.

Mark and Michael's chapter resulted from a felicitous collaboration made possible by computer technology. Joe Janangelo's story, of less felicitous collaboration, examines a new technology used for one of the oldest purposes on earth. Through the story of Orlando and Hedy, Joe explores how the new technology of computers engages tutor and writer in a dance around an old technology, the body. Joe registers a range of responses to Hedy and Orlando's exploits, from outrage, to reflection, to reexamination. He ends by speculating that the forcible removal of sexuality from all endeavors pedagogical has made the erotic seem unnecessarily prurient. His story of sexual exploitation in the writing center computer lab ends by suggesting that the recuperation of sexuality may lead to greater awareness of the forces at play in the academy.

Joe offers a challenge to the common assumption that the erotic and pedagogical should always be separate. Kate Latterell challenges another common assumption—that student-centered pedagogy is always preferable in centers. Kate examines the gaps and disjunctures between student empowerment through liberatory discourse and the experiences of working with students in writing centers. In doing this, she rethinks the language of "student-centeredness" and the notion of "authority" in writing centers.

Throughout, her concern is not with the issues themselves, but rather with *how* the writing center community *talks about* the issues. She looks at the assumptions of student-centered tutoring, first through her experiences with Carlos and second through the narratives of feminist pedagogy.

What We've Concluded

The vivid and personal nature of these narratives seems in some ways the antithesis of acceptable academic prose. The irony we discovered, however, is that these stories bring to life some of the most academic of texts. The narrators in this volume have tightly tangled story and theory, making academic theory accessible, perhaps acceptable, and more authoritative. We want to use this volume of stories to argue for academic narrative not (only) because it is more humanistic, more humane, more "fun," but because it is rigorous and truthful. We want to suggest that stories can and should offer insights into theory, thus enlarging our concepts of the field. Through these stories we are able to glimpse the theories of Bakhtin, Cooper, Foucault, Holzman, Goffman, and Pratt in action—as interpretive frameworks for writing center experience.

It seems odd and sensible that story and theory can interanimate each other, making each more powerful. We believe that this power comes from the storytellers and returns to them, and to others like them who use stories to help themselves and others understand the nature of language, literacy, and learning.

1 A Story from the Center about Intertextuality and Incoherence

Lynn Craigue Briggs
Eastern Washington University

Several years and a worldview or two ago, I had a relationship with a writer at the writing center. This relationship turned many things on their heads for me—my romantic notions of writing, my sense of who I should be as a consultant, my acceptance of coherence as a standard of academic discourse.

Before I met Mary Ann I was a pretty good, pretty process-oriented writing center consultant. I believed in the dominant linear model of learning, consulting, writing. I believed in and followed the rules of my writing center: I filled out the forms, I completed sessions neatly in an hour, and I let the writer do most of the talking. My relationship with Mary Ann presented another model of learning, consulting, writing— a model of a web—and this model allowed me to break the rules, neglect the forms, and stay later in the center. My relationship with Mary Ann was productively disruptive, and reflection on it continues to be so. As a writer with much authority, Mary Ann made me feel empowered to make changes in my consulting—changes that weren't necessarily sanctioned by the Institution.

Initial Contact

Before Mary Ann came in for her first appointment at the writing center I checked the file drawer for her records—"No records, new writer." But when she showed up she didn't look new to me, she looked old, or older, at least, than most of the writers I worked with. She looked rather gray—wavy graying hair, neutral clothes, sort of pale. I introduced myself to her, wondering what brought her in, noticing the thick folder under her arm.

As a fitness-frenzied, newly pregnant, twenty-five-year-old doctoral student, her age, her grayness were things I dreaded for myself. I was consciously aware, in my condition and position, of trying to remain lively, colorful, and young.

Our dual (or duelling) folders stood as symbols of the expectations each held for our meeting, our relationship. In mine were the slips of paper that defined our center as a writer-centered place within a university that valued recordkeeping, checks, balances, and procedure. As a representative of the center, the one carrying the folder, I implicitly brought in those values.

We sat down in the little windowless room. I took out my folder, she put hers aside. My rules and procedure-governed agenda took precedence, I claimed my authority as university representative. I took control of the agenda—I gave her forms to fill out, waited until she completed them, and began the consulting protocol. I asked her how she had heard about the center. She indicated that her friend Marjorie—a really interesting character, eighty-six years old and writing a historical novel on ancient Greece—had recommended she come in. Since Mary Ann lacked the immediate charm of being eighty-six, I was sort of put off. Although I had been charmed by her friend Marjorie's idiosyncratic visits, I was used to anxious undergrads or eager grad students, whose institutional needs seemed to make them trusting of me. I was used to writers who didn't do self-sponsored writing, who were writing because they were assigned it by someone who had power over them, writers who called me in as an intermediary, who acquiesced to me some power in the academy.

But Mary Ann looked like a housewife-poet. That, in my moments of angst, was my fear for my own life: that I'd end up as someone trapped inside someone else's economic support, dying for an expression of self. I was scared that she was like me and attracted to the possibility of alliance. I had hardly even spoken to her, yet I was tangled up with her already.

When she pulled her text out I was relieved to see that it wasn't poetry; it looked like letters. I asked her what she was writing them for. She said herself, then she said she wanted to publish them. I felt more comfortable with that. I liked the idea of having a goal. I was good at rhetorical problem-solving. I wasn't sure I could get into providing fulfillment for a homemaker who wanted strokes for her writing, but I could easily talk about streamlining and assessing audiences for publication. I was soothed. I could do what I had been conditioned to do—help a writer create a coherent text for an audience who had power over her. I didn't have to abandon my training and values to this woman who seemed so strangely like me yet glaringly different. I asked her to tell me more about her text.

She told me that it was a series of letters to her dead mother. I was put off again. I was annoyed. Wasn't this a waste of my talents? I was scared. What if she veered off into the heavily existential? I wasn't trained to deal with that. She indicated that it was a variation on a journal, a way of exploring issues in her life. I was worried about how personal this sounded. I liked working with writers who had essays to interpret or data to analyze.

Mary Ann seemed to think that I could give her feedback on this blurry discourse form. I had my doubts. I thought I was a good consultant because I was a good writer. But I was a good academic writer. I didn't even read fiction—just essays, studies, reviews. That was the kind of writing that got things done in the world. The kind that got people ahead. That is what I knew about and helped people with. After all, most of the writers I worked with wanted to get ahead, and saw writing as something they needed to master in order to do so.

I explained our procedures—that the writer reads to the consultant, that the consultant takes notes, that either can interrupt and ask questions, etc. I told her that we "work with the writer, not just the writing," a rather romantic notion at that time, in a center steeped then in process pedagogy as a way to accomplish the academy's agenda. I then asked if she minded if I taped the session, because I was doing a little research on the center.

"What kind of research?" she wanted to know. I explained that I'd change her name, that it wasn't about her text. That wasn't what she wondered about—she wanted to know my research methodology, my paradigm. I was surprised, but I stumbled through my then limited understanding of qualitative research and symbolic interactionism. She said that she had been drawn to qualitative herself, but in her field, of course, quantitative had been the norm.

And what was her field?

Oh, social psychology. She earned her Ph.D. from Chicago and had been a professor at a local college until . . . and then she said that I could certainly tape the session, and took her text out to begin.

As I had outlined in our procedures, she read the text to me. I was comfortable that she was adhering to the prescribed routine, but I was surprised by the text. It was personal right from the start. I was amazed at what she made known in her text so quickly—that her husband had cancer, that her mother was abusive, that she was a Quaker, that she suffered from manic depression, that she had two children, that her father was still alive, and that she was struggling with much in her life.

The pressure was back on me, I thought. My head throbbed. I'd have trouble not being affirming to someone with so much to bear, someone whom I thought might be fragile. I was exceptionally nice and delicate with my responses that session. It wasn't so much that I didn't really believe what I said, but I cut off my awareness of what I could believe. I had put a box around my potential negative reactions. I started by keeping them only to myself, then I stopped letting myself acknowledge them at all. I didn't want to disrupt her. The personal nature of the text and her investment in it made me feel as if I could be disruptive. And being disruptive in this way wasn't what I thought consulting was about.

Suddenly and ironically, Mary Ann challenged my sense of authority just because of who she was—she was or had been nearly everything I wanted to be. Funny, only moments before she had seemed to be everything I dreaded becoming. But as she described her accomplishments I saw that in the world outside of the center she certainly had higher status. Yet, she came to me for help. I felt that the way for me to achieve what I wanted in life—motherhood, a doctorate, a faculty position, higher status—was to do right by her. That made me feel under the gun, gave me performance anxiety when working with her.

Instead of feeling like I was with a writer who looked to me as the One Who Knows, I looked at her in that way. She was the One Who Knows dissertation writing and defense, employment, childbirth . . .

She left, and signed up for another appointment at the same time the next week. I was flattered—here was this really smart, older, professional person who wanted to work with me again. From my graduate student perspective, that was really reassuring. Apparently I had been a good enough consultant.

She came back the next week, and the week after that, and the week after that. She wrote and revised each week, and her thick folder of writing got thicker, even though we only got through about five pages a session.

As we worked I was conscious of being torn, of separating parts of myself as I listened to the text. On the one hand, I was the analytical, critical consultant-listener, taking copious notes, carefully tracing patterns, listening for skipped references, needed details, themes that tied sections together. On the other hand, I was my curious self, getting swept away, wanting to ask questions like "What do Quakers believe?", "How did it feel to be locked in an institution?", or "How long does your husband have to live?" I kept these voices in my head quiet, much as I learned to silence the negative reactions I had to her text. I believed that neither my negative reactions nor my personal questions were appropriate for my position and aspirations as a consultant.

I was also my concerned self, wondering if she was okay, if the friends she mentioned, or the relatives still living, or the Quaker community could support her enough when she needed it.

I was also my reflective self, thinking about my own relationship with my mother, and the relationship-to-be with the child I was then carrying. But I mostly talked from my consultant self.

For only one of these selves was validated by the academy—it was only appropriate for me to be my analytical consultant self in the center. I felt that this was the self I was supposed to be, the self I could talk about to other consultants after the session. I couldn't talk about the impulses of my curious self, for every culture I've been a part of has emphasized the need for privacy, the impoliteness of prying. My concerned self was also on the outs; after all, this was a person of more status and power than I. Wouldn't it be improper to suggest that she needed me to take care of her? My reflective self usually got stuffed until I was alone again.

But, somehow, she made me call on all of these selves, all of these voices. She forced me to use parts of myself that didn't normally interact.

But I mostly talked from my safer consultant self. I also continued to tape. Around this time my adviser exclaimed "This (a study of the consulting talk) is your dissertation!" I plunged into the relationship with a new investment. This wasn't just a nice woman with interesting stories anymore, this was my ticket to professional, economic, and social respect. I could finish my degree and have a baby—I could collect my data now and write between feedings and changes. Life made sense.

Yes, I was mercenary. I had a new commitment to the consulting relationship because it could get me what I wanted. It also seemed sensible to study this relationship. Already I was experiencing the tension that indicated that I didn't quite or always understand what was going on. It made sense in my well-conditioned academic schema to study something that didn't fit in with my conceptual framework, to use information to get control of it, to examine and analyze was a way to put my demons to rest. I later wondered: is careful study, research, coming up with a "better" understanding of phenomena how academics (and by cumulative association, the academy) get power?

I told Mary Ann that she was my dissertation. She seemed as delighted as I was. I handed the transcripts and preliminary analysis to the professor teaching my research class. He asked me to stay after class the day he handed them back. He said I couldn't do a study in which I was a part. I started to cry. Really hard. He said that it was too difficult for a first study. I cried harder and told him I was pregnant— by way of apology. He acquiesced to some degree and said that I could finish this project for the course, but that I would see that it was too hard to do for a dissertation.

I told Mary Ann. She disagreed. She really thought that it was fine to do a study in which I was part—she thought "objectivity" was a myth and a stupid thing to grasp at, anyway. I agreed. I felt supported. After all, Many Ann was a researcher, a former professor, a graduate of a really good school. And, I found out shortly thereafter, she was a friend of my dean. I learned that after I went to his funeral. He had the same kind of cancer her husband had. I swallowed hard when I heard that.

It was funny, my willingness to follow the rules of research that she laid down instead of those asserted by my professor. It was funny not only because I had transferred the authority over my dissertation to the subject of my dissertation, but also because in my rigid little writing consultant role I was buying into the same academic values espoused by my professor. I accepted them as consultant, rejected them as student. I was challenging the academic establishment, kind of like Mary Ann was challenging academic establishment—except when it came to the establishment I called home. I still followed or at least anguished over consulting rules.

She kept coming, I kept taping, but I also continued transcribing. Often when she would come I would begin the session by telling her something I had noticed in her text after I heard it on the tape. I would sometimes bring notes on insights I had had between our meetings. Sometimes I talked as much as she did. I violated several center rules: I set the agenda and did more talking, I stayed more than an hour, I failed to complete all the paperwork. I had made those rules in my administrative capacity. I felt guilty and justified at the same time. I was not doing what was supposed to be right, but I was doing the right thing. It seemed to be a more real relationship than the writing center rules had bargained for. But I needed her to keep coming back—she was my dissertation. She was also becoming a friend of sorts—sort of a big-sister friend, a mentor. In each session she would ask me about the progress of the project, offer insights, tell stories about the writing of her own dissertation, and spur me on.

Time for Evolution

Sometime into the second semester of our relationship I noticed that I made sure that I scheduled someone to come in right after her so that

I couldn't stay for more than an hour. Once she cancelled, and I felt relieved. I felt pressured when she was on her way in, and I worried that I wouldn't have anything smart enough to say. I was starting to weary of seeing the same sections over and over again, of debating the nuances of another revision. After five months of work I was impatient to get through the whole text and to get the damn thing out to publishers. I wanted to see that I had made a tangible difference in her writing process. After all, she hadn't shipped it off without me. I was thrilled when we got to the back of the folder, then disappointed when she had written more and revised again for the next session.

About this time she brought in her quilts. Big quilts. She had wanted to bring them in sooner but they had been displayed at the local museum. There were bags and sticks and liners—this was complicated, these things were works of art. She told me about the tradition each quilt had come out of, which letters she had been writing when she made which quilt, and what had inspired her decisions in the quilts. I was nervous when she brought them in, nervous in the same way I was when I was asked to talk about someone's poem or painting. As she unwrapped them I was scared that all I would see would be bedspreads. But I didn't. I was impressed and moved that she brought them in. We didn't talk about writing much that day, and we didn't tape. And I didn't secretly hope that she would cancel anymore.

Wall-to-wall quilts, bright and primal. I felt like I saw the color in them that I missed in Mary Ann the first day we met. I got a new sense of her vibrance that day. I valued vibrance, and, seeing that we shared that value made her seem less alien to me.

By sharing her quilts she had calmed me. Perhaps it was that I saw that she had another creative outlet, another area of tangible competence, and so could withstand a little negative reaction from me. I also stopped fearing that I wouldn't have anything to say, for I found it easy to talk about and interpret the quilts. These were colorful, abstract, geometric things, some of them Escher-like in their layers of complexity. I liked that we could turn them around and get different things out of them, that although she did have an idea of how she wanted them to be hung, she wasn't opposed to me viewing them upside down, or turning them over and looking at how the stitching made patterns on the back, too. The quilts—the "comforters"—eased my fear.

By bringing in her quilts, Mary Ann provided me with a metaphor to break me out of my linear model, values, and expectations of writers, writing, and consulting. These webs of fabric had multiple points of connection within them: I could turn them around (even over) and upside down and see different things. The quilts were nonlinear, yet connected. They relaxed me into an understanding of discourse that didn't depend on linearity for sense . . . that valued connection instead of simply coherence. This metaphor prepared me for another that arose when I stepped back from our relationship—the metaphor of a web. Mary Ann's quilts were like a tactile representation of the web of readers that would appear after we stopped consulting and I started analyzing our talk.

After Mary Ann brought in the quilts, I found my due date fast approaching. She started making two appointments per week. I appreciated this, for I felt like I needed the data (even though I already had hundreds of pages) and she seemed to feel like she needed to finish, too. Our consulting relationship ended abruptly when I delivered. I had hoped to continue it on a limited basis, but I had a noisy son who saw two hours as the limit for continuous sleep. I was sleep deprived, and walked past my data watching it gather dust.

Eventually I caught enough shut-eye to try to round out my dissertation committee and write a proposal. I had two committee members on board and enthusiastic. I approached a faculty member with whom I had been developing a relationship. I asked him if he would read my proposal and consider being on the committee. He said he would be glad to. When he read it, however, he was outraged. He told me that I couldn't do a dissertation in which I was featured, and that I'd need to scrap this whole idea and start over. He even went to my department chair and asked if he knew what I was doing. My chair replied that he knew, and thought it was a fine and important idea. I then recognized that I'd written some fighting words.

My son grew large enough to sit on my lap as I wrote and revised. One night while we were engaged in the battle over which one of us would get to hit the keys, the phone rang. It was Mary Ann. She wanted to know how my pregnancy had ended (nearly a year before) and to tell me that her husband had died. We talked for about an hour. It was odd talking to someone whom I had thought so deeply about nearly every day. Besides the fact that her voice sounded different on the phone and I couldn't make eye contact, I found that the Mary Ann I was constructing for my study—in effect my fantasy Mary Ann—didn't exactly match the person on the phone. She said some things I didn't expect. I guess I thought that after all that transcribing and categorizing I would be able to anticipate her words, actions, reactions. It seemed strange that she could surprise me.

I thought about her in a variety of ways. I thought about her text, as I encountered pieces of it in my analysis of our talk. I thought about her life and her loss. I thought that maybe she would come back to the center now that I was working again. I thought about her as the writer I was constructing in my study.

About another year later I called her. I said that I was going to present on our research relationship at a conference, talking about the considerations, complications, and consequences of practitioner research. I wanted her input on my talk. I went to her house to present it to her. All I wanted her to say was "Good. That is how I remembered it also." She didn't, of course. I realized I had trained her to be a good consultant. She retold me what I had said, she asked questions, she gave her reactions and traced them to the text. I had to revise, I knew. I wasn't very happy.

A year after that she called me. This time, I had just suffered a loss. My father had just died. I invited her to lunch. We made small talk and didn't discuss anything of substance, although there had been such substantial changes in our lives. Our children, whom we brought together for the first time, seemed to annoy each other. We were trapped inside by a torrential downpour which set the scene. Perhaps we were disappointed that being together couldn't magically evoke the ethos of the previous time, before the disruptive deaths.

I had anticipated more consonance than dissonance in our luncheon meeting, but it was just the opposite. I thought that after all the study I would really have a handle on our relationship.

Relationship as Document

Shortly after graduation I was hired as an assistant professor in my graduating department, charged with directing the center. My office was a converted session room—the bigger of the two that Mary Ann and I had occupied—the one she had laid out the quilts in. Every time I unlocked that door I felt her behind me; in the beginning I would sometimes turn around to usher her in first. Although she wasn't really there, she really was. And my relationship with her showed me how many others were in that office, and were in that room every time we consulted.

There are so many things I learned with Mary Ann, about consulting, about research, about being a woman at the academy. I can't speculate on all of them, but I'd like to focus on a couple of lessons, a few connections, and a question or two that this whole episode left me with.

The Web of Readers

When Mary Ann and I would meet, one of the things we would talk about was how to get her book published. I often brought this around to the concrete things that I was familiar with, and the things that I could help her control. One of these things was audience. I asked often whom she wanted to read her book. This question led to lots of different answers, from "women," to "people who want to get better," to those who would be shopping in a religious bookstore, looking next to Leo Buscaglia. We both constructed this audience, with me asking "how about" questions, and her filling in details. Although the details sometimes changed from week to week, one thing that didn't change was that when we talked about the people who would read her book, we always talked about them in general, demographic terms.

Though this audience was amorphous, it had an impact on the text and on my reading of it. As we would construct, deconstruct, and reconstruct the target audience, I would change my slant on the text. When we had constructed the audience as people with religious interests, I would not speak up if I felt like the text was too heavily or confusingly spiritual. When the focus was on women I would feel free to say what I thought. As the readers who were constructed moved closer to me and farther away, my approach and focus shifted. That "general audience" for the book, those people to whom we had never put faces, affected how I was able to read, what feedback I provided, and therefore the information that Mary Ann had when she revised.

But the general audience wasn't the only group to crowd into the consulting room. Mary Ann was a great reader, and she would often compare her work to that of other authors. She talked about being repulsed by a Judi Chicago piece, about being envious of Ann Morrow Lindbergh's style, about having a goal similar to Carol Gilligan. As a result of her descriptions of these authors (and the fact that they weren't familiar to me) I started to read around. I borrowed the Lindbergh book from my mother-in-law. I asked about Judi Chicago. I had lunch with a friend who was using Gilligan's book in her class. I found out about authors she mentioned, and I brought my knowledge to the sessions. Sometimes I was so proud that I had done my homework that I would begin the session with a description of what I had found out.

My knowledge of these other authors influenced my consulting too. I initially felt ignorant, like a student, like I was shirking my "consultantly" responsibility by not knowing them. Then when I did some investigation I saw Mary Ann's text differently—no longer did I see it as this idiosyncratic piece, I could now trace it to a tradition. I could put her text in perspective, I could see it, and respond to it, in a new light. I didn't feel like I was captive of her words anymore—I had new knowledge of some rhetorical traditions to lean on. I could hear echoes of Lindbergh's reflective style, of Gilligan's themes. Mary Ann's work didn't seem so isolated and new to me after I had sampled the work of those other authors.

By learning about and from the other authors Mary Ann drew from I became acquainted with her intertext (Porter 1986), the traditions and sources Mary Ann was immersed in and familiar with. I saw that it was these echoes and traces of other authors' work that made it possible for Mary Ann to creatively borrow her way to an "original" text.

It was with regard to other authors that Mary Ann turned the consulting tables most sharply. We had been chatting regularly about my dissertation progress, but that wasn't the focus of the session, until one day when she brought me a book to read. It was called something like *Reflections of a Woman Anthropologist*, and it dealt with ethical issues—such as distance to subjects—and research paradigms. We talked that day about her renunciation of her membership in APA. She had decided that the APA paradigm—with what then were heavy quantitative pressures—conflicted with her values. That was an eye-opener for me, the notion that research approaches weren't neutral, and that by virtue of the way I chose to pursue our research relationship I was defining and declaring my values. It seemed that I needed to step back and consider what my values were, and what I wanted out of my study.

When I returned to consultation after that session I wasn't the sort of naive practitioner-researcher of the previous weeks. I had thought some about what I wanted, what mattered. I started being a little more reflective and critical of my methods and behaviors. I stopped telling writers that what was important was what they wanted to say—as if they were writing in isolation. I wanted to know what the discourse communities, those others in their intertext, wanted, expected, and contributed. Those other authors in our relationship brought me to that.

But she didn't just bring other authors into the sessions with her, she brought her friends, her relatives, her husband. No, not literally, but she brought their readings, their reactions. I reacted to those reactions. I argued with Wendy's approach (it was very different from mine), I agreed with Becky's, I dismissed Roger's. We spent lots of time weighing and processing what they had said. It was one of these real readers who was responsible for her bringing in the quilts—P. J. had told her that her writing was like quilting. I inquired about that comment— P. J. said that Mary Ann used the same process when quilting— drafting, literally stepping back, and then revising—as she did when writing. After I asked, in came the quilts. The quilt session was an important one for me in understanding my role as consultant.

After Mary Ann shared her other real readers' reactions with me, I was aware that I was reading her text in a public forum. Although we hadn't much discussed her other real readers' reactions to my reactions, it was clear that she had shared them on occasion. The door to the consulting room seemed so open, allowing people to pass in and out. That door became the door to my office.

It was not only when I opened the door to my office that the echoes of my relationship with Mary Ann haunted and inspired me. I think about her and what I learned from the relationship frequently. One of the gifts that the relationship gave me was insight into theory, and a way out of my romantic vision of writing/reading/consulting. My relationship with Mary Ann allowed me to touch the heretofore theoretical intertext, and forced me to abandon any vision of the writer as an individual creating in isolation.

A while later, as I was preparing to analyze the transcripts of our sessions for my dissertation, I read Marilyn Cooper's "The Ecology of Writing" (1986). Cooper describes how interconnected readers and writers are, and how the production of a text sends cascades of reaction through a discourse community. She presents an illustration of how a friendly holiday memo from a boss reverberates through the web of employees and affects other texts which follow it. Cooper's metaphor of the web of readers hit me. That was what we were constructing in our sessions. The folks we brought to life—the general audience, the other authors, the real readers—they were the web that Cooper describes, and they had a profound impact on both of us and on the text. I wanted to jump up and down. I had never "seen" theory like that before. The references to these people were in the transcripts—black and white, names and characteristics. They were there, and I could trace the way that they mattered.

It was a kind of creepy realization—we were not alone in that room. Like Mary Ann's mother, who haunted her to the point of composition, the others in our web of readers hung over us. It was, in fact, very crowded with people we could not and did not abandon. The impact of the others in the web of readers that we spun was real, tangible, textual. It was not an ephemeral notion that our texts, our reading, our writing, were shaped by the others to whose language we were connected.

I realized that although my relationship with Mary Ann was unusual, it probably wasn't unique in this respect. Probably every session I had had or could ever have was tainted by the echoes of others. Some echoes were from recent exchanges—the students who came in to redraft after bloody feedback from their instructors—and some echoes were from the past—my recollections of how respondents had helped (or not) my writing. I understood that I was never alone with the writer in those sessions, that the writing center could never be a garret (Lunsford 1991), for there were no individual geniuses coming in, only writers with a whole lot of connections in their webs.

Porter's text further helped me eliminate any fantasy that I had about nurturing the individual writers and teasing out creative geniuses. It wasn't my role or my hope any longer to try to get the writers to dig deep into their souls. Instead I wanted the writers to look around at their intertext. I wanted to engage writers in discussions about how they came to where they were, what they valued, and where they believed they could go. I wanted them to identify, acknowledge, and listen to their web of readers . . . to be comforted and inspired the way that the quilts had inspired me.

Together in Coherence

Except.

Except listening and acknowledging and responding to such a raucous and diverse crowd would be confusing. If writers listened to all those voices and wrote for them, texts wouldn't be coherent. They'd be messy, divergent, multivocal in response.

I myself heard but did not listen equally to all the voices ventriloquated in the room. I chose to attend to and align with those voices that were consonant with my values. And my values, at that time, were largely mainstream academic values. And academics, I believed then and believe now, value coherence—to the point that I would call academe the "culture of coherence," where coherence is expected from academic, and especially student, texts.

But if I listened to all the voices I heard and wrote for them all, and encouraged other writers to listen and write, it would be wrong, wouldn't it? It would go against my mission of helping writers to write "better." Perhaps it wouldn't be wrong, but it would be antiacademic. I would go against all I had been socialized to be as a writer, consultant, writing teacher. Coherence was king where I came from. And like a king—male, powerful—it meted out material rewards and punishments.

So, I wondered, what was the right thing to do? To encourage writers to streamline, to unify, to jettison divergent ideas in order to meet the expectations of those who insist on coherence? Or should I support exploration, multivocality, messiness, chaos, learning—all that stuff that gets texts labelled "incoherent?"

The culture of coherence began to scare me when I noticed how insidious it was. In my work with faculty and writers across the curriculum I often heard yearnings for coherence, condemnation of things that were not coherent, without a hint of interest in why they were not, what it might mean that they were not, and what could be gained if they were not.

It dawned on me that in academe "coherence" wasn't seen as a construct, as an option, it was seen as the way, the truth, and the light. It was parallel to the stance I perceive in those enmeshed in the current traditional paradigm. I would argue that one of the characteristics of that paradigm is that participants don't recognize it as a paradigm. It was the same with coherence. Who would question it?

Perhaps the only folks who could be incoherent and respected as writers were the poets. As my chagrin when I constructed Mary Ann as a housewife-poet attests, I had been conditioned to see this kind of writing as less serious, less important, less interesting, less manageable. The incoherence of poetry and the idea of working with a poet made me uncomfortable. I was indoctrinated into the culture of coherence. I was an agent. A secret agent, maybe, and the secret was kept from me, because at that point I didn't see it as a construct either.

But is it a secret whose voices get listened to? In the journals, the textbooks, the manuals for writers, coherence is exalted. Try submitting a multivocal text for publication to a research journal. When I did, the responses were not pretty. Try advocating chaos and discovery for student writers. The other faculty members at the meeting will not be pleased. The need for texts to be coherent means certain dangerous things probably can't get said. They won't be published. They don't fit into the expectations of the discourse community.

I want to question the culture of coherence, and to suggest that its days may be numbered. I hope that the reified, deified construct of coherence becomes an option and not a requirement, so that ideas that are too broad, too divergent, too "both/and" to fit into coherent texts see the publicity of print. Let academic prose come closer to poetry—the poetry I feared as a consultant.

I know that I have looked upon coherence as a sign of mastery—a sign that my student has been indoctrinated, also. It is also a shortcut for me. If a writer produces a coherent text, I don't have to work as hard to create sense. That is expeditious when there are a few dozen papers in the stack. I have judged coherent writers as having control over the material as well as the discourse. And I have rewarded control—when I have been in control of the situation enough to do so.

But the model of consulting I started with—the rather romantic model—urged me to give away my control, to let the writer be in control. As Alice Gillam (1991) points out, though, having one person or the other in control of the session, assuming that one voice must dominate, is univocal. However, after the quilts, when I started to hear the other voices (albeit selectively) the sessions became more multivocal. As our relationship became real, control was less of an issue for me. I stopped consciously acquiescing to Mary Ann's agenda. I stopped stopping my negative response. I stopped pushing toward publishable coherence.

I have since come to the conclusion that the breaks with my indoctrination that my relationship with Mary Ann allowed came in part from her status as a postsocialized writer and academic. Mary Ann came to the center with real world power, and comfortable and confident in that power, she could break the rules without fear. And I, torn between two powerful sources, two sources of power, Mary Ann and the institution, largely strode the middle road. But the door had been unbolted by my relationship with Mary Ann, and I was beginning to see what was inside. I saw constructs and values, paradigms and choices, not truths, commandments, or laws.

The Future in Coherence

I have been heartened recently as I have looked at metaphors provided by technology. Two software pieces, HyperText and PacerForum, stand out for me as media that embrace incoherence, and perhaps provide not only a metaphor but a means for the crumbling of the culture of coherence.

HyperText allows nonlinear insertions into linear text—insertions which are signaled onscreen with a cursor and can be taken up or ignored by a reader. PacerForum allows online conversations between multiple users, with many users responding to a prompt at the same moment, and thus, because of the real-time lag between the writing and reading all the users are doing, creates a text with thematic relationships, but not linear ones. Maybe as technologies and attitudes evolve, composition students will be encouraged to create texts that are like humus—rich, messy, synthetic, and fertile.

If these increasingly popular and accessible technologies support and celebrate incoherence, perhaps the unquestioned reign of coherence will end. Perhaps, as academics begin to recognize the inconsistencies between these technologies and the status quo, coherence will no longer be recognized as the truth, but only as a rhetorical option.

"Don't Be So Sure"

My relationship with Mary Ann shook up many of my assumptions—assumptions about writing, pedagogy, the academy, and discourse. Perhaps the most significant thing shaken was my understanding of the nature of knowledge. My consulting relationship with Mary Ann shook the foundations of what I thought I was expert at. This relationship suggested the value and necessity of questioning my assumptions. I fully expect my assumptions to be challenged again. I think that my work with Mary Ann has enabled me to better recognize such a challenge when it comes along. Whether she actually said it, or whether I put these words in her mouth to sum up our relationship, I can hear Mary Ann's voice saying "don't be so sure." I think that those are apt words for me to live by in my academic life.

Works Cited

Cooper, Marilyn. 1986. "The Ecology of Writing." *College English* 48 (April): 364–75.

Gillam, Alice M. 1991. "Writing Center Ecology: A Bakhtinian Perspective." *Writing Center Journal* 12 (Spring): 3–11.

Lunsford, Andrea. 1991. "Collaboration, Control, and the Idea of a Writing Center." *Writing Center Journal* 12: 1 (Fall): 3–10.

Porter, James E. 1986. "Intertextuality and the Discourse Community." *Rhetoric Review* 5.1: 34–47.

2 Intellectual Tug-of-War: Snapshots of Life in the Center

Elizabeth H. Boquet
Fairfield University

Just as I sat down to write this paper, a student came up to me for help. She was exasperated, as novice computer workers and uncertain writers often are in the writing center: "My paper won't print out and I need to leave now."

I hurried over to the printer and checked to make sure it was online. Everything seemed to be in order, but still her paper wouldn't print out. Rather than have her wait while I looked into the problem further, I suggested to her that she move to a computer that printed at another station. She replied, "I don't care what you do."

When I asked her what she wanted to call the file so that we could save it, she said, "I don't care what you call it." So I saved it and moved to another computer, yet when I went to call up the file I discovered a maze of subdirectories with no trace of the file that I had just saved. When I asked her if she had been working in a subdirectory, she almost blew up: "Just give me the disk. Just give it back to me. I don't have time to mess with this. I'm just not going to do it."

She grabbed the disk from me, tore through the writing center and slammed into an international student who was waiting to be tutored. Since all the other tutors were busy, I sat down with the ESL student and asked him how I could help him. "Could you check my grammar?"

"Sure," I wanted to reply in my most cynical voice, "Why not." Instead, I mustered up all the charm I had left at 8:30 on a Monday night and sat down to work with what I hoped would be the last of a seemingly endless stream of students that evening. I was tired. I was cranky. I had other work to do. But all those things were not this student's fault. Above all, I had to remember that.

These are scary things to admit. Will my readers think that I'm a bad tutor? Or worse, a horrible person? Should I instead talk about the things I've done right in the center, about the tasks I know I can perform well? That temptation is great, but it is not, for me at least, as

17

necessary as analyzing the moments when tutors do things "wrong," either intentionally or unintentionally. Nor is it as worthwhile as examining moments when tutors are simply at a loss, as I was when the student mentioned earlier stormed away, leaving me standing there in a cloud of dust. So this paper will be about those moments when tutors feel that their own progress toward becoming the "ideal" writing center tutor is jeopardized.

The World as a Stage

For many tutors (including myself), working in a writing center is their first "real" job. In his book *The Presentation of Self in Everyday Life* (1959), Erving Goffmann supplies us with a reading of the world as a stage that might help us to envision life in the center. As tutors, our performers are stepping into a role for which an ideal already exists. As represented in the literature on writing centers, tutors are supportive; they are peers; they affirm; they question. These are formidable expectations for beginning (or for any) tutors to fulfill. Part of the problem seems to be that, with few notable exceptions (*The Writing Lab Newsletter* and the National Conference on Peer Tutoring and Writing being the most obvious), conclusions are drawn *about* peer tutors, information is produced *for* peer tutors, but rarely are these things created *by* peer tutors. Tutors are often objectified and essentialized in the literature devoted to them. In this way, tutors are disallowed a voice in the literature that pertains most directly to them. Even though many tutors have several semesters of training in composition theory and several years of experience tutoring, they cannot, almost by definition, be considered professionals. A peer is *not* a professional; a tutor is *not* a teacher. This is the pro and the con of the job. John Trimbur writes, "[N]ew tutors are already implicated in a system that makes the words "peer" and "tutor" appear to be a contradiction in terms. . . . [T]o be selected as a peer tutor in the first place seems only to confirm the contradiction in terms by acknowledging differences between the tutors and their tutees. . . . Appointment to tutor, after all, invests a certain institutional authority in the tutors that their tutees have not earned" (1987, 23). How far such authority extends, however, is not always clear, thereby causing the tutor to sometimes feel torn or confused about her role in the writing center.

In fact, tutors' authority even within the tutoring sessions they conduct has been suspect, as evidenced by the fact that, until recently, tutors have been disallowed a voice in the tutoring sessions they conduct. Much of the standard advice about tutoring, with its gene-sis in Vygotsky's zone of proximal development and psycholinguis-tic theories of bootstrapping, emphasizes the need for tutors to "mirror" students' questions back to them so the students can engage in *self*-discovery. Some practitioners, like Brooks in his 1991 article "Minimalist Tutoring: Making the Student Do All the Work," appear downright militant in their insistence that tutors refrain from engag-ing in meaningful dialogue about a student's text. Interesting that a discipline emphasizing the social nature of knowledge-creation brings us right back to the individual.

Although I certainly wouldn't wrestle authority away from the writ-ers themselves, I also know that simply reflecting student concerns back to the student does not always foster the most productive tutorial envi-ronment. I don't want students to perceive me as having all the answers, yet very often I do have the answers they are looking for, and the stu-dents themselves know it. While I know that, in the ideal tutoring situation, I (as tutor) would facilitate a student's self-discovery, I also know that real tutorial cases are not always as simple as that. ESL stu-dents usually come in looking for help with their grammar, sentence structure, and punctuation. This is often not knowledge that I can help them access, because it is probably not knowledge that they have. By attempting to have them figure it out for themselves, I end up feeling as though I've perpetuated the very notion that I am attempting to dis-pel—that there is a body of knowledge "out there" that some people (like me) have access to and other people (like them) do not.

In an unpublished essay entitled "Pedagogy of the _____: Resisting Secrecy in College English Classrooms," John Tassoni states, "[A]s teachers we need to avoid moments . . . in which information and opinions are withheld in ways that jeopardize creativity and undermine democratic relations in the classroom" (1). He argues that such secrecy merely serves to "hypostatize knowledge and reinforce unfair power relations between teachers and students" (1). I would argue that such secrecy, particularly as advocated in writing centers, can also be a self-preservation device. It is yet another way of justify-ing our existence to the faculty and administration, of assuring the powers-that-be (whoever they may be) that we don't "give away any answers." And by engaging in such a practice, we fail to educate our students, our tutors, our colleagues, ourselves. What is the justifica-tion for ostensibly creating spaces in which dialogue can occur only to encourage our tutors to be anti-dialogic? What sort of message are we sending to the students we tutor if they perceive us as withhold-ing information vital to their academic success? And to the tutors trained in the writing center, most of whom will take their places (and their philosophies on teaching) into classrooms of their own?

Until now, most of the talk on tutor-training has focused on the overt curriculum—the articles tutors are given to read, the sessions facilitated by directors, the courses designed for tutor development. Much of the training taking place in the writing center, however, falls more in line with Giroux's notion of the hidden curriculum. Tutors are generally intelligent people who quickly learn that the reality of life in the center is much different from that most often depicted in journals. They see that even experienced tutors fade into the woodwork of the writing center (or, as was the case in one writing center, sneak off to the bathroom) when they simply can't face one more student, leaving other tutors to pick up the slack. Through these observations, tutors learn that, when they applied for a job at the writing center, they agreed to join a team whose members are concerned with what Goffmann calls "impression management": "Within the walls of a social establishment we find a team of performers who cooperate to present to an audience a given definition of the situation. . . . Among members of the team we find that familiarity prevails, solidarity is likely to develop, and that secrets that could give the show away are shared and kept" (239).

Breeding a sense of solidarity is crucial to the success of any writing center team, yet, particularly in the writing center, the division between performer and audience is not always clear. Living in our postmodern era of splintered subjectivities, we know that it is not as simple as saying that tutors are performing for an audience of students. Subject and object coexist in a relationship much more dynamic than their binary rhetorical opposition suggests. And tutors themselves are not blank slates. They must negotiate the role of tutor so that it squares with the other roles they play in our society, roles marked perhaps by race, class, gender, and sexual orientation, to name a few. At the same time tutors feel an obligation to back each other up, to make the performance succeed. Tutors defend each other to students, directors defend tutors to professors, and tutors defend professors to students. These are precarious positions, since no one is ever fully a member of any one group. As Goffmann writes, "[W]e must be prepared to see that the impression of reality fostered by a performance is a delicate, fragile thing" (56). The director, for example, is a member of the writing center team, but is also an arm of the administration. The tutors are peer tutors, at once in solidarity with the students and spokespeople for academia. According to contemporary ethnographers, no longer is it fashionable, or useful, to view workers as static, as worked on by their environments. Instead, we need to view workers as dynamic forces within their workplaces, as actively shaping as well as being shaped by their surroundings (Hodson 1991). This tug-of-war can prove to be an enabling force, a means of asserting a self, especially in the writing center.

On Stage with Michael

Learning how and when to assert that self is tricky business. As a graduate student in a rhetoric and linguistics program, I tutored students whose professors frequently had less training in (and less interest in) teaching composition than I did. One of my students, Michael, came in during the first week of classes with a packet of worksheets that his professor put together. It consisted of symbols that stood for propositions, assertions, contradictions, etc. He showed it to me and asked me to help him decipher it. I couldn't. He seemed dismayed. He explained to me that he was to write two sentences per night, following the format described by these symbols, and by the end of the semester he would have a paper.

I was astounded, speechless. There I was, at a university with one of the oldest Ph.D. programs in composition in the country, and that legacy meant very little in terms of pedagogical methods even within our own department.

Michael wondered aloud if all English classes were like that. I smiled weakly and raised my eyebrows. He said, "I have friends who are taking English classes, and they're not having nearly as much trouble as I am." I didn't know what to say. I was caught between my knowledge as a professional, my responsibility to students, and my precarious position as a graduate assistant in an ancillary university service. What would have constituted stepping out of bounds? This student has the right to know that he is not getting his money's worth (literally). I have an obligation as a member of this profession to attempt to effect change within it, yet I feel powerless. And I wonder when I will ever feel power-full. When I have a "real" job? When I have tenure? When I'm a full professor? And I have to ask, along with Carroll, Carse, and Trefzer, "How can we hope to participate in the transformation of the profession . . . when we are ourselves in the process of transformation, struggling to create professional selves in an institution that marginalizes us while dictating the shape of those future selves?" (1993, 64). In this way, perhaps, the profession ensures, by means of subtle (and not-so-subtle) coercion, that its members fall short of the ideal.

In the incident with Michael, I decided to comply with the expectations set out by our writing center directors concerning faculty-tutor-student protocol. In other words, I kept quiet and helped the student as best I could to perform the tasks required of him within the confines of the class. At the time, I justified my actions by reminding myself that the "ideal" tutor is to be neither a student-advocate nor a teacher-advocate. Rather, my job as a tutor was to help Michael learn to operate within the constraints of his rhetorical context. And the instructor, obviously, was a large part of that context.

After a bit of soul-searching, I realized that I hadn't been completely honest, either with Michael or with myself. As a tutor, I was not perched on the fence of neutrality. By failing to speak to this situation in any meaningful way, I was, in fact, aligning myself with the faculty. Politically, I couldn't afford to make an enemy of a faculty member, and I didn't want to put the writing center director in the position of having to defend me (and by default, to defend the writing center) to this faculty member, to the department head, and possibly even to the dean. By comparison, failing to empower a student seemed like a small price to pay. Nevertheless, I don't know how I would have done it differently. I only know that I never felt more acutely that I had fallen short of my own "ideal."

Tutoring as Work

In my interaction with Michael, I acted out the script as it was written for me by the institution—no improvisation allowed. Other tutors with whom I've worked have become quite skilled at quiet subversion. The narrative that I would like to retell involves one tutor who used the very documents intended to record writing center activity to control the ways in which she was written into the center's history.

Tutors, like all workers, strive for situations in which they are able to exert some measure of control, of dominance, over the systems at work on them. Attempting to explore this issue, Randy Hodson conducted an ethnography, the results of which are published in his article, "The Active Worker: Compliance and Autonomy at the Workplace" (1991). Hodson concludes that "workers are active on their own terms and as motivated by their own agendas. These agendas are much more diverse than those theoretically allowed them by management theory or radical social science theory and include both compliance and resistance as well as autonomous creative effort to structure their own work" (47). One of our tutors, whom I'll call Shelly, embodied this compliance and resistance whenever she was faced with recording her tutoring sessions.

Shelly was wonderful with students. Her quiet, calm demeanor drew students naturally to her, and she was quick to tutor any student who needed help. Sometimes in the course of one afternoon she would work with six or seven students. So I found it quite odd that, as I was going through our files, her name rarely showed up as having tutored any of the students that we had on record. When I asked her about this, she replied, "I never fill those sheets out. They take too much time. If the student wants a note sent to her professor, I'll send that, but other than that, I just don't worry about it."

Our writing center is fairly high-tech, with over thirty IBM-compatible computers, but there is one thing that, despite all our technology, we cannot avoid: paperwork. We fill out forms (or we're supposed to) on every student we tutor. At the first staff meeting, we are told that these forms are extremely important to the success of the writing center. They prove our usefulness institutionally. They compose us. The more students we service, the more satisfied customers we produce, the more funding we receive. As is often the case, economics becomes the bottom line, and writing center administrators, like the tutors to whom they serve as mentors, are forced to make decisions and compromises, some of which they are happy with, some of which they merely tolerate.

This emphasis on documentation proves problematic on many levels. As Hurlbert and Blitz write, "[D]ocuments and the literacy demands they contain teach us our place(s) within the institution, institutionalize us, (con)figure us into the autobiography of the institution, incorporate us, make us part of the institution's scene. They tell us what to do and where to do it as they describe, for us, what we *are* doing" (1993, 6). This focus on accountability leaves us subject to the judgments of administrators who may understand little about the idea of a writing center (as North sets it out in his 1984 essay "The Idea of a Writing Center"). Moreover, it places us squarely in the middle of a quantitative tradition of justification that few of us believe in. To perceive ourselves as being "allowed" to exist by some external force as long as we prove ourselves "worthy" is to live with the constant threat of extinction.

To ward off extinction, we use these forms to represent our client base. They write the students that we tutor, reducing a dynamic interpersonal exchange to a mimeographed sheet full of circles and checks. Susan Miller's point about the grading system seems applicable here as well: "In the case of the student, grades and a record of them will be kept to identify and describe that student as an object of the 'grading system'" (1991, 90).

What remains unsaid, however, is that these forms are there for the tutors' protection as well. It is to their benefit to record a particularly difficult session, or one that they feel was significant in any way, in case they need to justify their actions to the student who receives a poor grade, to the professor who feels a particular paper does not represent the caliber of the student's work, and on up the institutional ladder. In other words, they are to note sessions that are less than "ideal" or that stray from the norm in any way, for these are suspect.

Tutoring without Offense

Creating spaces for dialogue arguably does increase the chance for such "suspect" sessions to occur. In my own experience, those students with whom I have abandoned the traditional tutorial model in favor of a more genuine exchange of ideas have frequently been the ones who caused me to question my own value as a tutor. Radical educational and cultural theorists advise us to "teach the debate" (Graff) and to view our cultural spaces (whether in the classroom or the writing center) as contact zones, "social spaces where cultures meet, clash, and grapple with each other" (Pratt 1991, 34). Pratt reminds us that too often we teach with the goal of eliminating confusion, opposition, and discomfort when our goal should be to delve more deeply into these issues. This, of course, does not always make for pretty sessions—struggles rarely are. Certainly, this is a problematic position to advocate for writing center tutors, many of whom are gaining their initial teaching experience in the writing center. But it does seem to be the appropriate time to advocate that tutors interrogate their practices responsibly from the outset and to recognize "pedagogy as a form of cultural production rather than as the transmission of a particular skill, body of knowledge, or set of values" (Giroux 1992, 202).

I learned this lesson the hard way with Tom, a nontraditional student who greeted me every Wednesday night at 6:00 P.M. sharp. Tom was just back from the Gulf War, anxious to pick up where he left off. In his research writing class students were allowed to choose a theme according to their interest and focus all their papers on this theme. Tom chose the death penalty. Tom is a Republican. I am not. We went round and round about his papers, but he kept coming back for more. One typical session began when he said, "This paper is entitled 'Should Juveniles Be Executed?'"

I was offended already, but I suggested that he read the paper aloud to me. As he read, it became apparent that he was not examining whether or not juveniles should be executed. Instead, he was trying to decide whether or not they should be *called* juveniles. In his conclusion, he decided that we should not sentence juveniles to die. Rather, any juvenile who commits a crime severe enough to warrant the death penalty should be *called* an adult and *then* sentenced to die. I began the session by trying to point out to him that the issue he was really debating was a semantic one. After I stated my case, he tried to back off: "Look, it doesn't matter to me one way or the other. All I'm saying here is that we shouldn't kill a kid unless that kid does something so bad that an adult could be killed for it."

I replied, "It's obvious you don't care about the issue, and if you don't care about what you're saying, why should your readers care? Your job as a writer is to make me care about what you're saying." At this, he became furious: "Why should I care? He (the professor) doesn't care. You're saying you don't care. Who does care? All I want to do is get out of this class, and no matter what I do it's not right. Just tell me what I need to do, and I'll do it."

How tempting. And the more difficult a session is, the more I want to just tell the student how I would write the paper. Mark Hurlbert uses Althusser's work to

> [help] tutors become aware that their practices are textured by an institutionalized, educational ideology that sanctions certain discursive forms while excluding others. This ideology can lead a tutor to appropriate a student's text, to make it look and sound like an institutionally sanctioned text. . . . In this case the tutor is no longer offering options, he or she is, despite their best intentions, institutionalizing composing and is reproducing the conditions of production as they are set out by educational ideology. (1987, 6)

Writing tutors, perhaps more than any other students in the university, are the students who have mastered the discourse and internalized the ideology of the institution. To the students they work with, tutors embody the university's ideal. So it is only fitting that those same tutors, often unknowingly, serve as the instruments through which that discourse is enforced. When they are affectionately called the "the cream of the crop," these tutors usually take this appellation as the highest of all compliments, but they should also realize that this makes them among "the most indoctrinated part of the population . . . the ones most susceptible to propaganda." As members of the educated class, they are "'ideological managers,' complicit in 'controlling all the organized flow of information'" (Chomsky, in Olson and Faigley 1991, 19).

The tutor, then, is an arm of the educational establishment, monitoring and regulating production. Tom, by indicating his reluctance to invest himself too heavily in his writing, was questioning the very foundations upon which our discipline rests. Students do this frequently, complaining, "This is stupid. Why do I have to do this?" Yet tutors rarely feel compelled to answer. Is this because they can't? Is this because they want students to question, but only within acceptable limits? Many writing center tutors want students to begin to look at how their subjectivity is constructed, but not too closely. Miller observes, "[This] may involve the student in freely choosing among topics for writing so that questions about the universal requirement 'to write' at all, or about the purposes for 'writing' essays, will be begged" (89–90).

Even though I did not address Tom's question about the purposes behind his writing assignments, I would like to think that, despite our differences, Tom's tutoring sessions with me were, for the most part, productive and engaging. This has not been the case at all times and with all students. Most tutors are all too familiar with that sinking feeling that indicates a tutoring session gone seriously amiss. My most memorable such encounter occurred with a student whom I'll call Joe.

The phone rang on a Monday morning early in the semester. The student on the other end of the phone asked, "Do I need an appointment to see a tutor?" I replied that no, he did not need an appointment to meet with someone. We take students on a walk-in basis. Ten minutes later, he walked in and we sat down to begin going over his paper.

Joe was a young, working-class kid already embittered by what he perceived to be the injustices involved with being white and male in our society. I took a deep breath and braced myself for the session as he began to read his paper aloud. He claimed that minorities have it easy because all they have to do is shout "Discrimination!" and women have it easy because all they have to do is shout "Sexual harassment!", but white men have no recourse when they are not happy with their situations. He also asserted, in the midst of the Clarence Thomas hearings and the William Kennedy Smith trial, that the court systems are "female based."

Where to begin? I contemplated honing in on the derogatory terms he used to describe certain ethnic groups, but then I realized this approach was just cosmetic. Changing those terms wouldn't change his prejudice, and there were more pressing problems with the organization and content of the paper that I technically should have been worried about. I began to question him about the logic of his paper, faulting him, for example, for only citing one personal instance of his experience in a "female-based" court. I challenged him that for every instance he could think of where the court system was female based, I could give him three instances to prove that it wasn't. At this point, I realized I was out of line and pulled back. I was no longer helping him to grow, either as a person or a writer. In fact, I was on the verge of attacking him.

He looked small and tired as he said, "I had a feeling this would offend you." I told him that I was sorry but I just couldn't help him with this paper. Fortunately (for him), we had a white male tutor who was willing to pick up where I left off. But I was left with the knowledge that I had failed as a tutor. Not only could I not help Joe with his writing, I probably served to reinforce the very prejudices he was clinging to so dearly.

Deciding when, how, and even whether to criticize student opinions has been a constant battle for me. I realize that I ask students with dissenting opinions to offer much more evidence for their positions than I ever expect of students with whom I agree. I, like other composition specialists, see it as my job to encourage students to begin to question their assumptions. Yet I wonder where to draw the line? It's one thing to ask students to look at their values, quite another to force them (by way of a grade) to change their opinions. What have we really accomplished if all of our students become like Tom, so frustrated that they will write anything just to have the grueling process over with? Does writing as discovery still mean discovering what the teacher wants and writing it?

Susan Miller claims, "Society produces fairly well-constrained subjectivities to regulate and map individuals. Regulation includes ways to instill values and responsibilities that best serve the society's maintenance of its particular form of order" (90). Individual variations in subject positions produce my reading and Joe's reading of discrimination, but who am I to say that my reading is "correct," when correctness is so arbitrary? Chomsky would say that my notions of correctness are typical of the "academic left," a term which is truly a misnomer. He asserts that the academic left in America is not left at all. It too is institutionalized, maintaining the appearance of dissent. Consequently, there really exists no radical extreme in America. My reading of an issue is as culturally determined as Joe's is.

From this last incident springs a joke that circulated among the other tutors in our writing center: if a student came in with a paper topic that was particularly offensive to us, we would save that student for Bill, our politically incorrect tutor. Writing in favor of capital punishment? See Bill. Pro-Life? Talk to Bill. And perhaps most importantly, since most of our tutors were female, sexist? You'll have to wait for Bill.

During my tenure in the writing center, Bill served as a frequent reminder that tutor-student relationships are not the only ones that fall short of the ideal; tutor-tutor relationships can run aground as well. Bill often managed to avoid tutoring because he knew so much about the computers, and he would lord this knowledge over the other tutors. When I began working at the writing center, I knew nothing about computers, so I was reluctant to confront Bill about his attitude when I relied so heavily on his knowledge. By the end of the semester, however, I was tired of the way he treated people, women in particular. My anger peaked when I heard him lie to our director about having taught one of the female tutors how to use the graphics program. I confronted Bill, telling him in no uncertain terms that I had been a witness to the initial exchange. He had not taught her anything. He had done it for her. I accused him of behaving this way in order to maintain some measure of control and dominance over other people. I then calmed down enough to explain why this was not only unacceptable but offensive to me. He said that he would try to be more considerate in the future, and he was—to me.

Bill's actions seem to be consistent with sociolinguistic analyses of language, gender, and power. As Tannen points out in her book *You Just Don't Understand: Women and Men in Conversation* (1990), men's communicative strategies are primarily hierarchical while women focus on connectedness. For this reason, women are more likely to involve others in operations involving them, while men are more likely to view a teaching situation like the one described above as an opportunity to assert dominance and control (67). By excluding the female tutor from the process of creating the graphics, Bill was playing directly into this stereotype.

Because he knew so much about computers, Bill did very little tutoring of writing. Those sessions he did concede to do, however, were very directive, and his students were reluctant to ask him for more help when he seemed so impatient with them. Frequently, they would purposefully seek out a female tutor for further clarification, reinforcing the split between domineering male tutors and their more empathetic female counterparts, between the men who are comfortable doing most of the talking and the women who engage in active listening. This reading is consistent with the findings of gender and language studies conducted by researchers such as Fishman and Aries, who found women to be more willing to engage in conversational maintenance work (giving backchannel cues, asking questions, nodding their heads) and men to be more likely to dictate topics, beginnings, and endings. Women fulfill a primarily enabling role, providing an open, supportive environment that is preferable to both men and women. With the female tutors engaged in the more service-oriented work, the male tutors were left to attend to the mechanics of the center's operation—fixing the printers, retrieving lost files, etc.—thereby reinforcing the traditional gender stereotypes. Again, Tannen says that we can view this in terms of a hierarchy: "Mutual understanding is symmetrical, and this symmetry contributes to a sense of community. But giving advice is asymmetrical. It frames the advice giver as more knowledgeable, more reasonable, more in control—in a word, one-up" (53).

Life in the writing center thrives on such asymmetry, and on the hope that we can eventually achieve some sort of symmetry, if not harmony. As I look back over these snapshots of life in the center, I realize that the pervasive feeling of often being at a loss, unable to do much good, stems from a desire to foster such connectedness, a goal which, as Miller and others have pointed out, has historically prevented composition practitioners from advancing institutionally (42). We are loath to fill out forms that take our time away from others who are waiting for our help; we are reluctant to talk to computers when we would prefer to talk to people; and we have difficulty working with people who perpetuate stereotypes which we know are damaging to others.

Perhaps the greatest dis-ease I feel is not easily captured in a vignette depicting life in the writing center. It is larger than that, resulting from the perception that writing centers exist on the margin of the margins. The field of composition is marginalized within the university, serving as a gatekeeping device where students must prove they are worthy of higher education (Miller 85), but writing center students are not even considered worthy of composition. This is a view rooted in ignorance, as anyone who has worked in a writing center can attest. Writing centers represent "the marriage of what are arguably the two most powerful contemporary perspectives on teaching writing; first, that writing most usefully is viewed as a process; and second, that writing curricula need to be student-centered. This new writing center, then, defines its province not in terms of some curriculum, but in terms of the writers it serves" (North 1984, 438).

Perhaps North is right; but the goal of the educational institution, as Jeanne Simpson has noted, is often simply one of survival. Helping students as we do in the writing center is the means of achieving what at times seems to be a less than altruistic end. In *Zen and the Art of Motorcycle Maintenance* (1975), Robert Pirsig alludes to a kind of "systematic thinking" that is institutionally pervasive. He writes, "To speak of certain government and establishment institutions as 'the system' is to speak correctly. . . . They are sustained by structural relationships even when they have lost all other meaning and purpose. . . . The true system, the real system, is our present construction of systematic thought itself, rationality itself" (94). Our educational system, based as it is on the industrial model, has production as its ultimate goal. We might not change that. But we can control *what* we (re)produce. We can strive to produce better writers, better tutors, more humane working conditions for everyone involved (tutors and students alike).

Then we can stand back and realize that we have a product we can
all be proud of.

Works Cited

Aries, Elizabeth. 1976. "Interaction Patterns and Themes in Male, Female, and
    Mixed Groups." *Small Group Behavior* 7.1: 7–18.
Brooks, Jeff. 1991. "Minimalist Tutoring: Making the Student Do All the Work."
    The Writing Lab Newsletter 15.6: 1–4.
Carroll, Shireen, Wendy Carse, and Annette Trefzer. 1993. "Fashioning Profes-
    sional Selves." *Critical Matrix* 7.1: 63–79.
Fishman, Pamela. "Interaction: The Work Women Do." *Social Problems* 25.4:
    397–406.
Giroux, Henry A. 1992. "Resisting Difference: Cultural Studies and the Dis-
    course of Critical Pedagogy." In *Cultural Studies*. Ed. Lawrence Grossberg,
    Cary Nelson, and Paula A. Treichler, 199–212.
Goffmann, Erving. 1959. *The Presentation of Self in Everyday Life*. New York:
    Doubleday.
Hodson, Randy. 1991. "The Active Worker: Compliance and Autonomy at the
    Workplace." *Journal of Contemporary Ethnography* 20.1 (April): 47–78.
Hurlbert, C. Mark. 1987. "Ideology, Process and Subjectivity: The Role of
    Hermeneutics in the Writing Conference." Paper presented at the Annual
    Meeting of the Conference on College Composition and Communication,
    Atlanta, 20 March. ED289161. 2–14.
Hurlbert, C. Mark, and Michael Blitz. 1992. "The Institution('s) Lives!" Marx
    and Rhetoric. Special issue of *Pre/Text: A Journal of Rhetorical Theory*. Eds.
    James A. Berlin and John Trimbur. 13.1–2 (Spring/Summer): 59–78.
Miller, Susan. 1991. *Textual Carnivals: The Politics of Composition*. Carbondale:
    Southern Illinois University Press.
North, Stephen M. 1984. "The Idea of a Writing Center." *College English* 46.5
    (September): 433–46.
Olson, Gary A., and Lester Faigley. 1991. "Language, Politics, and Composi-
    tion: A Conversation with Noam Chomsky." *Journal of Advanced Composition*
    11.1 (Winter): 1–35.
Pratt, Mary Louise. 1991. "Arts of the Contact Zone." *Profession '91*, 33–40.
Pirsig, Robert M. 1975. *Zen and the Art of Motorcycle Maintenance*. New York: Ban-
    tam Books.
Tannen, Deborah. 1990. *You Just Don't Understand: Women and Men in Conver-
    sation*. New York: Morrow.
Tassoni, John. "Pedagogy of the _____: Resisting Secrecy in College
    English Classrooms." Unpublished manuscript.
Trimbur, John. 1987. "Peer Tutoring: A Contradiction in Terms?" *Writing Cen-
    ter Journal* 7.2 (Spring/Summer): 21–28.

3 Marginal Comments on Writers' Texts: The Status of the Commenter as a Factor in Writing Center Tutorials

Patricia A. Dunn
Illinois State University

Recently I heard through the grapevine that I am "too soft on grammar." It is said that as director of the writing center I do not insist enough on the eradication of comma splices, and that some of the peer tutors I've trained have occasionally failed to recognize several of these in the drafts of students who come to us for help. Such a criticism implies that to seek out and destroy comma splices is, or should be, one of the prime directives of the writing center, and that my main job as director is to make sure peer tutors are walking grammar textbooks—without acknowledging, of course, that such texts often conflict with each other, for political reasons, regarding usage. It implies further that tutors should take primary responsibility for perfecting writers' drafts, and that the director's job, therefore, is to make sure peer tutors are astute editors. When I heard that criticism, I knew that I and the complainer were on planets so far apart that communication between us was light years away.

The person lodging the complaint (not directly to me) is a tenured professor who sits on several powerful committees and votes on my tenure hearing next year. Although I have the full support of my division chair, and I continue my policy of training tutors to respond to writers rather than writing, to listen rather than lecture, and to address the comma splice only after other, more important issues have been addressed, I am uneasy about the rumors. Feeling like both a wimp and a hypocrite, I even spent a portion of our precious staff meeting time reviewing comma splices and making sure tutors could recognize them. If I had had equal status with this tenured colleague, would I have been as bothered by the criticism? I think not. Rather, I might have confronted him privately and perhaps had a collegial discussion of writing theory, usage controversies, and academic freedom. Perhaps I should have done that anyway. However, since I am a firm believer in

Freire's assertion that true dialogue cannot occur between people of unequal status,[1] I have chosen instead to write about it.

I am, however, uncomfortable writing this critique of my colleague for several reasons: first, because as a yet untenured person, I'm a little scared of stirring up trouble. Second, I feel pangs of cowardice knowing it's a lot easier to write about this in a collection he may never peruse than to go to his office tomorrow morning and talk with him. Third, I feel just a bit disloyal whining about a colleague who teaches in the same institution as I do, an institution that has always supported me and my ideas about the writing center, even if those ideas have departed from those of my more established colleagues. I must also admit that this particular professor, although his philosophy of assessment emphasizes different values than mine does, is just as entitled as I am to privilege those values in his assessment of writing.

This same professor marks as wrong students' use of *they* after a singular subject. I do not know if he discusses with his class the current controversy surrounding pronoun use, as written about in *College English* by Sharon Zuber and Ann M. Reed (1993). I do know that I've advised peer tutors to point out options regarding pronoun use and to discuss with writers the context and consequences of their choices, using as a point of departure the Zuber and Reed piece and other research discussed later in this essay. However, I'm always aware that the grapevine may report that "Professor Dunn says it's okay to use 'they' with a singular subject"—without the contextualized explanation. Does this bother me? Yes—more than I'd like to admit. My untenured status makes me feel vulnerable to the criticism of those with a different view of "correctness," especially if they also happen to be in a position to vote on my continued employment.

Before I get too involved, however, in complaining about my untenured status and using it as an excuse for uncomfortable choices I've made, I will tell another story. In this one, the marginal comments with which I disagreed were made by a person whose status is regarded as lower than mine: an adjunct instructor. As Donna Singleton points out, *adjunct* is a word that both denotes and connotes the negative, and it is only slightly preferable to a variety of insulting terms non–tenure track instructors are called (1991, 32–34). I suspect that my pedagogy in the following situation was also influenced by my position and that of the person making comments in the margin of the paper (and in the margins of the academy).

One day, I noticed that in the usually benign confusion of the writing center, a young woman was waiting her turn, her elbows propped on the table, holding up her scowling face. At our small, liberal arts college, some students, before they take English 101, must take a basic writing course, some sections of which are taught with the thesis-driven, five-paragraph theme as a centerpiece. Last fall, the writing center was very busy with students from this one basic writing class, the instructor of which not only featured the five-paragraph theme but also mandated that each student visit the writing center at least once a week. Already I had philosophical differences with these requirements, but at the moment I put them aside and sat down with this young woman, Tara. Tara sighed a lot.

Her paper was decorated with many marginal comments: admonitions to focus the thesis, to place it firmly in the first paragraph, and to not stray from it. There were also similar instructions to include a clear topic sentence at the beginning of each paragraph, as well as much prescriptive advice regarding what constituted appropriately specific examples. I instantly developed a profound distaste for the instructions I saw in the margins, and I sympathized with Tara's surliness. The satisfaction I felt at feeling superior to the voice I heard in these comments, however, was ruined by my remembering C. H. Knoblauch's and Lil Brannon's warning against attempting to judge comments out of context—without knowing the relationship between writer and instructor nor the specific classroom dynamic that launched the assignment (1981). I also knew that if another professor were casting aspersions on *my* comments to students without knowing the whole story of how they came to be there, I would not be pleased.

I did, however, know the teacher—a young instructor who taught five first-year writing courses, three at our college and two at a local community college. Although I disagreed with his policy of teaching the five-paragraph theme and of forcing his students to go to the writing center, I also knew that he believed in process writing, gave his students several opportunities to revise, and had a lot of confidence in peer tutoring. While I secretly questioned some of his requirements and commentary, I also marveled at the time he spent with students, the extensive comments he made on their papers, and his ability to remain good humored in spite of what must have been an exhausting teaching schedule.

The context in which I read these comments was different from the one described earlier involving the comments of the tenured professor. While I disagreed with the comma splice and pronoun use philosophy in the first situation, I did not feel free to directly criticize those comments or that professor. Now I was reading the comments of an adjunct instructor, with whom I had the luxury of feeling smug without feeling vulnerable to his opinion of me. While I still would not directly criticize his comments in front of his students and I had no power over him, as a tenure-track assistant professor I occupied a higher rung on the academic ladder than he did. He did not attend department meetings, let alone vote on my tenure.

His student's piece of writing was a comparison/contrast essay regarding living at home versus living on campus. She was supposed to have one thesis, which was to be spelled out decisively in the first paragraph and then supported in the following three. She readily saw that both living situations had their advantages and disadvantages. Her main point, as I gleaned it from her entire essay and from chatting with her, was that although living at home was comfortable and predictable, she preferred the sometimes uncomfortable, unpredictable dorm life because it made her more independent and mature.

The problem, at least in the confines of this assignment, was that she didn't say that in her first paragraph. There she wrote that living at home was better. Readers expecting to see a five-paragraph essay in which writers are told to put their "main idea" in the first paragraph would no doubt read that as her thesis. Her teacher may have drawn a diagram on the board and have been expecting her to follow that simplistic blueprint. Given that context, a reader, especially the teacher, would expect each subsequent paragraph following the "thesis" to provide examples supporting it. The writer's first two paragraphs did just that, but then she moved, albeit somewhat imperceptively, toward a different idea, which was that *in spite of* the comfort and security offered by life at home, life away from home was better because it pushed her toward independence and self-reliance.

However, that's not what she wrote. Her examples seemed to describe the kind of frightening yet exhilarating challenges living in the dorms provided, but she left them to speak for themselves. Because the instructor was searching for a thesis where he said to put it—in the first paragraph—he found one: that life at home was good. This assumption set up expectations that the rest of the essay would support that "thesis." What was missed by both student and teacher is that the writer's first draft was a way toward figuring out what she really felt about her living arrangements. It was during the process of writing that first draft that she worked her way toward a more complex idea, not yet completely formed.

If this tutorial were going to support the instructor's marginal comments, the tutor would help the writer generate more examples of why living at home was preferable and eliminate the examples which "strayed from the thesis." However, those rogue examples were the ones that supported her eventual thesis—that living in dorms, for all its problems, was preferable. It just took her a draft or two to arrive at this.

She, of course, had no interest in "supporting with examples" the idea that living at home was better. However, when she realized, through answers to my questions, that she really wanted to argue in favor of dorm life, she became a lot more eager to generate examples. The problem was how to manipulate this thesis to fit the thesis-sentence-in-first-paragraph form required. I thought her own original form, rhetorically, worked better. It made sense to begin with the comforts of home and then gradually show how the discomforts of dorm life were, in the long run, more conducive to emotional growth. I was in a dilemma. Should I go into a long explanation of how her original organization, with a few points of clarification built in, was a more natural and effective arrangement for what she was trying to argue? Should I jeopardize her grade by telling her to ignore the structure her instructor was insisting on?

Over the space of a few seconds, I wondered how I could approach this tutorial without having it become an old-fashioned power struggle—a gunfight at the OK Corral with the student caught in the crossfire. Was it possible to *both* support my colleague's marginal comments (as I think I would want mine supported) *and* supplement them so that the writer could make her own decisions? I have always relied on Peter Elbow's philosophy of "embracing contraries" to get me out of, or rather to keep me in the thick of, such dilemmas: "Affirming contradictions and not being in too much of a hurry to get rid of them . . . must be one of the patterns of thought that makes wise people wise" (Elbow 1986, 252).

We discussed options. She could keep the original "thesis" as her teacher interpreted it in her first draft—that home life was better—and follow his directions to simply add more examples as to why that was the case. A second option was to keep the same form—home life described first and how good it was, and then end with how much better (if problematical) dorm life was. We both knew, though, that the resulting paper would not fare well in grading—it wouldn't fit the prescription. The third option, the one she finally chose, was to put in her first paragraph something to the effect that in spite of the comfort of home life, dorm life, with all its problems, was preferable. From there, she could still keep her basic structure of discussing home life first, and then move into the evidence that dorm life was better.

Since her instructor required from the writing center some kind of documentation that his students came there, I used that opportunity to drop him a note explaining how this student really needed to change her thesis in this draft. As I wrote this note, I wondered about my role in this whole scenario and others similar to it. How did my decisions affect the writer? Did she receive a better grade because of the tutorial? Probably. But so what? Other questions haunted me: Did she leave with a better attitude toward writing? Will she experiment with how she organizes her future writing projects? Six months or five years from now, what will she remember about writing, drafting, and the nature of consultation and revision? If not required to secure a response to her writing, will she ever again set foot in a writing center?

Like the story related earlier, this one also concerns pedagogy and position, but in this one, I occupy a safer position than does the teacher. I wondered how peer tutors would have handled this session. More often than not, it was they who tutored this instructor's students. Would they have followed his advice in the margins to give more examples of the first paragraph's "thesis"? Were my options as a full-time, tenure-track assistant professor the same options open to undergraduate peer tutors? Could these twenty-year-old undergraduates, paid five dollars an hour, have written the same kind of note I did, essentially explaining why the instructor's marginal directions were not strictly followed? How would such a note from a peer tutor be received by the instructor? And did my relative comfort in challenging this instructor's marginal comments have anything to do with the fact that he was an adjunct and I was a full-time assistant professor? I wrote no such notes to my tenured colleague, and my objections to *his* pedagogy were based on more serious ethical questions. I was, and still am, deeply troubled by how many pedagogical decisions are based, at least somewhat, on my status in the academy and that of others.

Disagreements about five-paragraph themes, comma splices, and pronoun use may seem like trivial issues when compared to other problems in our field and in our world. But assumptions about their triviality and who gets to make those judgements are not trivial and may directly or indirectly affect such issues as academic freedom, critical thinking, and even the career choices of young people.

First of all, it is quite obvious but not often recognized that when tenured faculty members decide the employment fate of their untenured department members, and not vice versa, that untenured instructors do not have the same kind of academic freedom as do their more secure colleagues. When writing centers are run or staffed by those without tenure and criticized by those who have it, it is risky for directors to protest philosophical differences publicly. It can be done, of course, but only with much care and tact, while criticism of untenured people can be done with virtual impunity. The sometimes unequal status of classroom professor and writing center tutor (whether student or faculty) sets up, by unspoken decree, a situation in which it is assumed that the tutor will unquestionably support the marginal comments of the classroom instructor. While there are of course many problems involved in challenging those comments—for both tutors and writers—there are also sometimes problems in not doing so.

One such dilemma concerns the five-paragraph theme, which has been sufficiently critiqued in composition circles for, among other things, its deadening effect on thinking and creativity. Knoblauch and Brannon call the five-paragraph theme a "pseudo-genre" so rigid and intellectually deadening that it may do more harm than good (1984, 31). Nancy Mack and James Thomas Zebroski argue that the form of the five-paragraph theme reflects "a pseudoreality which is far removed from the pain of working-class students' everyday lives" (1991, 157). When viewed as one of an infinite number of ways to present an argument—one that is discovered and explored—the thesis-and-support essay can occasionally be a reader-friendly, effective tool. But it is only a heuristic, an artificial and culturally based pattern. As Knoblauch and Brannon point out, when it is taught as *the* way arguments are presented, it can be extremely harmful, giving a fraudulent idea of how people write and persuade.

However, in spite of the fact that few people admit to teaching the five-paragraph format, and graduate school discussions seem to proceed on the assumption that it is a long-extinct dinosaur, it is quite obvious to anyone in the "real world" of teaching in a university that the basic thesis-and-support structure remains a most influential shape in academic life. It is so pervasive, in fact, that students use it as an overlay on what they read, inflicting it on essays not even remotely near the five-paragraph theme in form.

Here is an example. Last fall, I linked my first-year writing course with an introductory political science course—everyone in my class was also enrolled in that class. We read, from a collection of essays on American government, a piece by Susan Faludi called "Blame it on Feminism" (1992). For the first twelve paragraphs of her essay, Faludi presents, in a tone thick with sarcasm, her opponents' views of what is wrong with women today. With bitter irony, she writes what "they" are saying: "Women are unhappy precisely because they are free. Women are enslaved by their own liberation" (49). In the second part of her essay, with a deft, one-sentence paragraph, Faludi asks, "But what 'equality' are all these authorities talking about?" (50). Following that question, she addresses each of the points raised by her opponents and for the remainder of the essay, twenty-six more paragraphs, argues persuasively against each one in turn.

By that time, for many of my students, it was too late. Told repeatedly in basic writing classes and perhaps elsewhere that a writer's "thesis" should appear dutifully in the first paragraph, preferably the last sentence, and then be "supported" in the subsequent paragraphs, these readers had already "found" Faludi's "thesis." Here is the last sentence of her first paragraph: "At last, women have received their full citizenship papers" (49). Students like Tara, trained to write in what they now believe to be *the* academic form, read essays expecting them to follow that structure. They read Faludi's first paragraph as a chiseled monolithic "thesis" and then mold the rest of her essay into a procrustian bed of "support." Faludi's essay, appearing, after all, in an academic textbook, must be an extended five-paragraph theme. There sat the last sentence of her first paragraph, and it certainly sounded like the statement of opinion, the "thesis" they had all been trained to write and to find. So they found it.

But they missed it. So powerful had been their thesis-and-support lessons that for these students, this revered template for reading and writing overshadowed Faludi's bitter and obvious irony. Regardless of what comes after an essayist's first paragraph, many students will continue to see it as an introduction and thesis. In attempting to read all essays as they've been taught to write them—extended five-paragraph themes—students may be hampering their reading comprehension as well as their ability to think critically. Instead of dutifully helping students "improve" their five-paragraph themes according to their instructors' advice, we need to somehow voice our objections to the entire enterprise. The question is how to do this without jeopardizing our students' best interest as well as our own.

Just as insistence on the five-paragraph form may be harmful to students' writing and reading, so may blind insistence on fixing "comma splices," "fragments," and other minutiae of "bad writing" without discussing contexts in which they are admissible or even desirable. For example, E. Annie Proulx's excellent novel *The Shipping News* (1993) is replete with such "errors," and that won a Pulitzer Prize.

Pronoun choice is, of course, a much more serious issue for anyone familiar with recent cognitive research, which is beginning to demonstrate that people's reading comprehension and even their concepts of themselves and others are indeed affected by the pronouns they read and use. In their essay "The Reader's Construction of Meaning: Cognitive Research on Gender and Comprehension," Mary Crawford and Roger Chaffin discuss some findings relevant to this debate. They summarize a project in which college students were given a passage to read. Half the students read the passage written in so-called generic style—the use of "he" to refer to the singular subject, in this case, "psychologist." The other half read the same passage, except that the sentences were constructed using inclusionary language. The subject was "psychologists" and the pronoun was "they," or if the subject was "psychologist," the pronouns were "he or she." There was a difference in the way men and women recalled the passage. The men who had read the passage with "the psychologist . . . he" construction had better recall than men who had read the passage with the "psychologists . . . they" or "the psychologist . . . he or she" construction. Women, on the other hand, had better recall when they read the inclusionary version ("they," "he or she") than when they read the "generic" version ("psychologist . . . he") (16). None of the subjects was aware of the purpose of the experiment or that there was a difference in pronouns. What the results seem to suggest is that people pay more attention to writing that seems to speak to them. Women performed more poorly on the exclusionary passage, disproving the claim that "he" includes both genders equally. Men did better on the "he" only passages, suggesting a higher level of concentration on writing they perceived, if only subconsciously, as being about men.

Other research shows similar results. John Gastil's 1990 experiments showed that for his subjects, college students, "they" is the most generic pronoun, producing both male and female images in readers' minds (638). Interestingly, Gastil found that although women undergraduates picture both males and females for "he/she" and "they," ". . . undergraduate males have a difficult time reading any generic term as gender neutral" (639). In other words, these male subjects envisioned male subjects even for the pronoun "they."[2]

As much research is beginning to show, pronoun use may not be a trivial matter after all, but an important part of one's view of the world and a way of broadening (or limiting) the perspectives of everyone. The supposedly generic "he/him" may be a kind of subliminal insult to women, giving a powerful message to both sexes that women are not fully human and really don't matter very much. It is not unrealistic to theorize that exclusionary language practices may be somewhat responsible for the low status of women worldwide.

That is why the routine circling in red of "they" after a singular subject so infuriates me when I see it on papers brought to the writing center, apparently with the expectation that we are to help writers "fix" such "errors." For me, this is not a grammatical nor even a pedagogical difference of opinion, but an ethical one. What pronoun is used in the sentence, "Each scientist has _____ own opinion" may affect the career choice and the self-esteem of the young person reading the sentence. While men get one message about future career options, women get quite another. Pronoun choice is an issue far more important than what is typically discussed in the pages of handbooks and should be debated publicly by all members of the academic community.

Although the writing center is a site where conflicts about teaching and learning become most obvious, they cannot be confined there. In a thirty- to sixty-minute tutorial, I cannot discuss with writers everything I'd like to about writing theory, perceptive reading, or the consequences of certain language practices. Questions of what is and is not "correct" regarding pronoun use, for example, and whose preferences will prevail, should not be restricted to writing classes and writing centers but should be aired across the disciplines in psychology, sociology, ethics, early childhood, and business courses. The five-paragraph essay, and similar creatures of the academic archives, along with the pedagogical assumptions from which they developed, demand interdisciplinary and intergenerational research and discussion.

Current research in Writing Across the Curriculum is beginning to address these kinds of pedagogical assumptions and how they affect what becomes professional discourse throughout and within the disciplines. Charles Bazerman, among many others (see also Gross, Hansen, Jolliffe, and Myers), shows that contrary to the impression disciplinary textbooks sometimes give, professionals in a particular discipline do not always agree either on the forms of argument acceptable in that field or on what constitutes acceptable evidence.

In *Shaping Written Knowledge* (1988), Bazerman shows how the form of the experimental report has evolved over the years, as it was shaped by the changing philosophy of the scientific discipline. He also shows how the form of the ethnography has been altered to reflect changing fundamental assumptions in the field of cultural anthropology (1992). As Daniel Mahala argues in his 1991 *College English* essay, students should be made privy to these intersections of theory and practice that occur across the disciplines and the clashes that sometimes occur there.

Even the boring five-paragraph theme (which is nevertheless boring into all aspects of academic life), should be a part of this debate. These discussions may become lively, for they involve deep-seated, fundamental beliefs about the nature of knowledge and learning, not to mention sometimes unacknowledged assumptions about gender roles and authority. Somehow, in spite of differences in status and degree of job security, all members of the academic community need to find the courage and the grace to discuss these important conflicts openly.

Notes

1. See Nan Elsasser and Vera John-Steiner's essay, in Works Cited, p. 47.
2. See also Frank and Anshen, and Bodine, in Works Cited.

Works Cited

Bazerman, Charles. 1992. "From Cultural Criticism to Disciplinary Participation: Living with Powerful Words." *Writing, Teaching, and Learning in the Disciplines.* Eds. Anne Herrington and Charles Moran. New York: MLA, 61–68.

———. 1988. *Shaping Written Knowledge: The Genre and Activity of the Experimental Article in Science.* Madison: University of Wisconsin Press.

Bazerman, Charles, and James Paradis, eds. 1991. *Textual Dynamics of the Professions: Historical and Contemporary Studies of Writing in Professional Communities.* Madison: University of Wisconsin Press.

Berthoff, Ann E. 1981. *The Making of Meaning: Metaphors, Models, and Maxims for Writing Teachers.* Upper Montclair, NJ: Boynton/Cook.

Bodine, Ann. 1975. "Sex Differentiation in Language." In *Language and Sex: Difference and Dominance.* Eds. Barrie Thorne and Nancy Henley. Rowley, MA: Newbury House, 131–51.

Britton, James. 1982. *Prospect and Retrospect: Selected Essays of James Britton.* Ed. Gordon M. Pradl. Upper Montclair, NJ: Boynton/Cook.

Crawford, Mary and Roger Chaffin. 1987. "The Reader's Construction of Meaning: Cognitive Research on Gender and Comprehension." In *Gender and Reading: Essays on Readers Texts, and Contexts.* Eds. Elizabeth A. Flynn and Patrocino P. Sweickart. Baltimore & London, Johns Hopkins UP, 3–30.

Elbow, Peter. 1986. *Embracing Contraries: Explorations in Learning and Teaching.* New York: Oxford University Press.

Elsasser, Nan, and Vera John-Steiner. 1987. "An Interactionist Approach to Advancing Literacy." In *Freire for the Classroom.* Ed. Ira Shor. Portsmouth, NH: Boynton/Cook.

Faludi, Susan. 1992. "Blame it on Feminism." *Mother Jones* September/October 1991. Excerpted from *Blacklash, The Undeclared War on American Women,* Crown Publishers. Reprinted in *American Government Annual Editions,* '92–'93. Ed. Bruce Stinebrickner. Guilford, CT: The Dushkin Publishing Group, 49–53 (page references are to reprint edition).

Frank, Francine, and Frank Anshen. 1983. *Language and the Sexes.* Albany: SUNY Press.

Gastil, John. 1990. "Generic Pronouns and Sexist Language: The Oxymoronic Character of Masculine Generics." *Sex Roles: A Journal of Research* 23. 11–12 (December): 629–43.

Gross, Alan G. 1991. "Does Rhetoric of Science Matter? The Case of the Floppy-Eared Rabbits." *College English* 53 (December): 933–43.

Hansen, Kristine. 1988. "Rhetoric and Epistemology in the Social Sciences: A Contrast of Two Representative Texts." In *Writing in Academic Disciplines*. Vol. 2 of *Advances in Writing Research*. Ed. David A. Jolliffe. Norwood, NJ: Ablex, 167–210.

Hurlbert, C. Mark, and Michael Blitz. 1991. *Composition and Resistance*. Portsmouth, NH: Heinemann Boynton/Cook.

Jolliffe, David A., ed. 1988. In *Writing in Academic Disciplines*. Vol. 2 of *Advances in Writing Research*. Norwood, NJ: Ablex.

Knoblauch, C. H., and Lil Brannon. 1984. *Rhetorical Traditions and the Teaching of Writing*. Upper Montclair, NJ: Boynton/Cook.

———. 1981. "Teacher Commentary on Student Writing: The State of Art." *Freshman English News* 10.2 (Fall): 1–3.

Mack, Nancy, and James Thomas Zebroski. 1991. "Transforming Composition: A Question of Privilege." In *Composition and Resistance*. Eds. C. Mark Hurlbert and Michael Blitz. Portsmouth, NH: Heinemann, Boynton/Cook, 154–64.

Mahala, Daniel. 1991. "Writing Utopias: Writing Across the Curriculum and the Promise of Reform." *College English* 53.7 (November): 773–89.

Myers, Greg. 1991. "Stories and Styles in Two Molecular Biology Review Articles." In *Textual Dynamics of the Professions: Historical and Contemporary Studies of Writing in Professional Communities*. Eds. Charles Bazerman and James Paradis. Madison: University of Wisconsin Press, 45–75.

Proulx, E. Annie. 1993. *The Shipping News*. New York: Scribner.

Singleton, Donna. 1991. "The Names We Resist: Revising Institutional Perceptions of the Nontenured." In *Composition and Resistance*. Eds. C. Mark Hurlbert and Michael Blitz. Portsmouth, NH: Heinemann, Boynton/Cook, 32–41.

Zuber, Sharon, and Ann M. Reed. 1993. "The Politics of Grammar Handbooks: Generic *He* and Singular *They*." *College English* (September): 515–30.

4 Tutoring in the "Contact Zone"

Janice M. Wolff
Saginaw Valley State University

I don't remember her name, but I remember her need: to pass a first-semester freshman composition course at Northern Illinois University. Her instructor escorted her to the writing center, a space with which she was unfamiliar, a social space that seemed foreboding. The student carried a four-page essay booklet, liberally overlaid with red ink. Her mouth was too-red with lipstick, and her bangs jutted heavenward. She was just one of many students who entered the confines of Northern Illinois University's writing center in hopes of revising unacceptable papers into "what she wants." That year I worked with a variety of students: another young woman whose essays seemed to deconstruct themselves in alternating sentences; the master's student in art who talked through a thesis about art therapy; the student who needed help writing essay exams, who also called me at the end of the semester, angry about the fact that he had received a B– on his exam—what sort of advice had I given him, anyway? All these students could tell stories about their experiences in the writing center; all have been constructed in the social spaces of the tutorial session. But it is the student with the high-flying bangs who represents my first year in the writing center. She, like the other students, was not only seeking help with writing, but she was also seeking a "safe house" in the university environment.

Two years later, I was teaching at Illinois Benedictine College in Lisle, Illinois, working in the space I considered a "safe house" for students and myself. My experience there produced more of my tutorial history: I became a bit more systematic—keeping files, photocopies, and a tutor's log—more data, more carefully archived. More than becoming an archivist, I began to work with a more defined student population: mostly inner-city black males, recruited to the college in the interest of diversity. Techniques that had generally worked for writing tutorials no longer applied; I had to work carefully to see that the student and I were actually speaking the same language. Students often regarded the

43

writing tutorial with suspicion and me with disdain. No safe house yet. They came with their papers, and we needed to find a way to talk about the writing. I met Trevor in this environment at Illinois Benedictine, and he and I worked to develop a useful way of talking about writing.

It is only in retrospect, after varied experiences in writing centers, that I came to read Mary Louise Pratt's theory of "contact zone," theory that made eminently good sense to me, theory that provides another metaphor by which to conceive of the writing tutorial. But more than metaphor, knowing contact zone theory might have allowed me better access to student discourse. Contact zone theory defines the writing center spaces, spaces that by default become a "zone"; turning those spaces into a safe house took a bit more conscious doing. By borrowing the anthropological term "contact zone," Pratt provides language by which to speak of the imaginary spaces where differing cultures meet, often cultures with language barriers. The notion of the contact zone, applied to early historical periods, periods of conquest and colonialism, seems to have its parallels in the classroom and in tutorial situations, those spaces where people of very different backgrounds come together. "Contact zone," as Mary Louise Pratt defines it, refers "to social spaces where cultures meet, clash, and grapple with each other, often in contexts of highly asymmetrical relations of power, such as colonialism, slavery, or their aftermaths as they are lived out in many parts of the world today" (1991, 34). Contact zone theory seemed a likely way to view the tutorials comprised of inner-city black males and myself, a white woman in her mid-forties who has never lived anywhere with sidewalks—one with a Ph.D., no less. The other element of Mary Louise Pratt's contact zone that seems equally valid is the idea of the tutorial as a "safe house"—a hard place to get to, but nonetheless worth the trip. Students so often feel themselves aliens in an alien land, but to negotiate the contact zone, to have an awareness of the treacherousness of the zone, is to understand that those same social spaces that are alien can become "spaces where groups can constitute themselves as horizontal, homogeneous, sovereign communities with high degrees of trust, shared understandings, temporary protection from legacies of oppression" (40).

The notions of the contact zone and the safe house are central and valuable to tutorials for writing. Many times a trained tutor, speaking a specialized language, meets with a student who speaks another specialized language, the language of her culture. Somehow they must find a way to speak about the writing at hand. I should pay homage to Rod Serling here . . . somehow, they find themselves in . . . *the contact zone.*

When Pratt speaks of the contact zone, she does so from a socio-linguistic perspective. Writing tutorials replicate the social spaces and the symmetrical relationships of power—tutor and tutee are not on a level playing field. But although a "contact zone" understanding of the tutorial situation emphasizes the imbalance of power and expertise, the tutorial has the potential for becoming a safe house in the rather dangerous environs of the academic institution, a social space where meaning can be made, where risk-free learning can take place. The writing center may be one of the few comfort zones remaining in the university, a place for students to decompress.

Pratt identifies the social spaces and the power relationships in the tutorial situation in a way that others have not quite seen. While Kenneth Bruffee and Stephen North both grant that the writing tutorial occupies a social space, and imply the asymmetrical relationships of power inherent in the tutorial, Muriel Harris gets closer to the idea of the safe house that the tutorial has the possibility of becoming.

Muriel Harris comes closer to Pratt's construction of the contact zone, implying an awareness of cultural differences between tutor and tutee, but neither Bruffee's collaborative project, nor North's epistemic position, nor Harris's contrastive approach tells the story of the writing tutorial the way Pratt tells it. When the tutor points out the differences between discourse conventions in student writing, contact zone discomfort occurs; at this point, contact zone "rage and incomprehension and pain" can arise. Tactful discussion of differences becomes critical if Pratt's "safe house" metaphor is ever to become more than an imaginary space. If Bruffee, North, and Harris show the trickiness and the complexities of the tutorial situation, Mary Louise Pratt helps us see the tutorial in light of the sociolinguistic metaphor of the contact zone, where both impossible and improbably joyous things happen.

If Pratt's contact zone writing is produced, the sort that she calls "autoethnographic," a text "in which people undertake to describe themselves in ways that engage with representations others have made of them" (35). In other words, the writing subject tries to present the self in the writing as the "other" already knows her . . . it is an act of appropriation of the language of power and influence. Very often the writing and the tutorial "constitute a marginalized group's point of entry into the dominant circuits of print culture" (35). The writing becomes a sort of circling around: "I'm telling you what you already have told me I am"; "I am describing to you the self you have constructed for me."

And isn't this what happens to students as they begin their work in the writing tutorial? Isn't the marginalization of students unmistakable when they are sent or encouraged to make use of the writing center? Isn't it often a writing tutorial that functions as the point of entry for the student into new academic discourses? And isn't it very difficult for a marginalized student to consider the tutorial a "safe house"? (And aren't writing centers themselves on the margins of the university?)

Pratt further characterizes the contact zone as the place where "along with rage, incomprehension, and pain, there [are] exhilarating moments of wonder and revelation, mutual understanding, and new wisdom—the joys of the contact zone" (39). In addition to the possibilities of being painful and problematic, the writing tutorial can also be the site of wonder, joy, and wisdom. The tutorial *can* be a safe house.

Here I return to Trevor, who was a student at Illinois Benedictine College during the fall semester of 1991. When he arrived at college billed as an at-risk student, measured by various testing implements, constructed by both the label and the testing procedure, Trevor was directed to enroll in study skills classes and a developmental writing course, and assigned to an instructional assistance program—all designed to improve retention of students such as Trevor.

In spite of all the risk factors, Trevor left inner-city Chicago and attended a small, liberal arts college, Illinois Benedictine, a school situated near affluent Naperville. Geographically, the school sat at College Avenue and Maple, but it was at the intersection of study skills classes, writing instruction, a basic course, a reading course, and tutorials that Trevor found himself. Those of us who taught these courses felt it our duty to construct Trevor in Other ways—ways that might help him signify in a "white social Christian" culture—or at least to reconstruct his writing, reading, and thinking processes. Trevor and other students from Chicago found themselves needing to translate their vernacular for the more suburban and scholarly. In fact, there was a certain pride in translating gang signals and language for "white-bread" types such as myself. During second semester, Trevor was a student in a repeat section of basic writing. It was in that class that he and some friends set me straight on what it means to rig one's thumbs on the waistband of one's pants, cowboy style: the gesture signifies that the person carries a handgun, is "packing." (So who has the power here? Guns are surely metonyms for power, figurative and literal. Will students give up the hardware, the midnight specials, for the power that grammar will grant? That's why writing centers tutor students in writing, isn't it? How many zones do students have to negotiate? Real battle zones.)

Illinois Benedictine, a school whose policy encouraged "diversity," and which actively sought students from nearby Chicago, became a contact zone itself, in the way that it became the site of diverse cultural groups coming together, meeting, learning to speak, and sometimes erupting in campus skirmishes. The recruitment process resulted in a central irony: the college actively sought inner-city students, but then termed their language use nonstandard and deficient, and worked to replace their language with academic discourse. Students from "the projects," whether "Henry Horner" or "Cabrini Green," soon learned that they were marginal speakers and writers—they became the "projects."

I first met Trevor that fall, when he was a student in my section of study skills. Quiet, kind, shy, a bit overweight, recruited to play football, Trevor complied with the assignments. I saw him from time to time in the learning center, too, and knew that he was attending instructional assistance meetings in order to get through an economics class. He complied. In the short writing tasks I was asking of the study skills students, Trevor met the assignments; he fulfilled the tasks in a crabbed hand, showed intelligence, and once in a while I would see a flash of rhetorical play. I knew he knew who had power and who did not, who was on the margins and who was not. But it was later in the semester that Trevor and I worked together in the tutorial spaces.

I liked Trevor a lot, and worried over the strong Black English Vernacular that his writing instructors treated as deficient. I had read recent analyses of BEV, particularly one article by June Jordan in which she and her class spent the semester describing the linguistic conventions of the dialect. I felt the richness of BEV to be Trevor's strength, but apparently other teachers were encouraging him to speak and write white newscaster language. Trevor found himself in the contact zone, where those who wielded power also issued the grades. I wrote about Trevor, just as I journal-wrote about other tutees of mine. Here's a transcription of a journal entry from November 18, 1991:

> Two tutorials today—two very different experiences, two that need some writing/recording/musing. The first was tutorial with Trevor B_____. It seems that I "inherited" him from Martin (an instructor for the developmental writing course) and then from Richard (the writing coordinator). Martin diagnosed two recurring problems in his paper—forgotten past tense markers on regular verbs and subj/verb agreement problems where parts of the verb "to be" were involved, i.e., "She were going," "I were leaving." Somehow, somewhere someone's attempted to teach Trevor the subjunctive and here is the residue, perhaps? (I speculate on possible instruction.)

"Inherited him from" speaks worlds about the way many students are bounced from tutor to tutor, and the tragedy here is that these are professionals, not minimally trained peer tutors. My analysis of Trevor's syntax points up the difference of language, of expertise, of power, and it underscores how hard we had to work to communicate in the contact zone.

> Anyway, after having him tell me about the assignment—to write about a bad experience—and after my reading that found the paper to be about "my most embarrassing moment," Trevor and I worked at the sentence level, converting all verbs in a sentence to past tense. He read out loud and stopped where he needed to insert "-ed;" I think many times he says them, but maybe that dialect voice is at work when he is composing. So it was tedious work— we shifted "mine" to "my" in a couple of places and I showed him where patterns formed the same sorts of constructions. (The Mina Shaughnessy in me.)

Again, I have the language with which to describe the gaffes in conventional written English, and can contrast them with the features of Black English Vernacular. This working at the sentence level reduced the both of us to a particle-level revision. We weren't writing; we were doing damage control.

> But I, of course, was taken with his rhetorical sense: (the woman in his essay) wore "silk stocking[s] (we had to supply the plural marker) and pump[s], not the Reebok pump." Now that's a cagey writer! Trevor verged on sexism or voyeurism as he ogled the secretary during the job interview (but that worked toward reader interest and pointed out his 17-year-old naivete) (would that he were aware of the naivete and played on it—maybe he is! And I didn't get it.), but I thought it wasn't the time for a discourse on political correctness. Maybe it should have been . . . Then at the end of the piece he had two fragments back to back. But before I noticed the fragmented nature of the two, I noticed four clauses, all parallel, that summed up the experience—a periodic sentence for sure! He needed only to supply subject and verb. I saw the parallel structure as a sign of his success, as an indication of growth as a writer! And he wrote the subject/verb that made it a full sentence.

Here I continue to write that Other language, to speak of plural markers—what must he have thought of my linguistic doublespeak? But in the midst of the clash of cultures, in the midst of contact zone power struggles, occurred some of the joy of the contact zone, some of the wonder that Pratt alludes to. The rhetorical flourishes that Trevor used indicated a writerly sensibility, an understanding of what a writer must do in order to keep a reader reading. I was lavish in my praise. And the periodic sentence, something I had language for and Trevor had intuition for, showed a sophisticated command of structure. He had managed these feats in the midst of contact zone pressures. The entry goes on with a description of the work Trevor needed to undertake.

The journal entry parallels what Pratt tells us about writing tutorials and the contact zone: that there are inherent problems when two people attempt to talk about writing—two people who come from different cultures, two people who occupy asymmetrical positions, one with the discourse of power and the other marginalized and with little language for talking about writing. A sidelight to this story is Trevor's admission to me that if he could just master the "common slice" that his writing problems would go away. More evidence of the marginalized trying to gain access to the discourse of the powerful, and the "heard" language becomes something other than what is intended. Funny, yes—"common slice" is hilarious, but it becomes a hopeful marker of what can be accomplished in the contact zone.

Pratt tells us that the contact zone and the work done within the contact zone can result in literate arts: students might produce "autoethnography, transculturation, critique, collaboration, bilingualism, mediation, parody, denunciation, imaginary dialogue, vernacular expression." Trevor's rhetorical ploy was to make use of vernacular expression: "not the Reebok pump . . ." But there is also the possibility of "miscomprehension, incomprehension, dead letters, unread manuscripts . . ." all are the "perils of writing in the contact zone." As I look over my transcribed conversations with Trevor, the perils of the contact zone are evident: "common slice" is certainly illustrative of "miscomprehension and incomprehension," yet his inclusion of the "Reebok pump" infuses the text with vernacular expression, a sense of parody, and even transculturation—a connecting of popular culture with the discourse.

Creating a safe house is the work that Trevor and I set about doing: we worked on creating a way to talk to one another; we worked at leveling the playing field; we worked to trust one another. Trevor began to understand that in the writing tutorial, he was free from any "legacies of oppression." Ultimately, writing center work needs to make the contact zone the site for safe houses. Pratt contends that the contact zone, with its triumphs and its perils, can become a safe house for students, whether that safe house is the classroom or the writing tutorial. The contact zone is a metaphor that works, that can illustrate something about the dynamics of the writing tutor's job; it defines both tutor and tutee, and marks out the cultural spaces for the conversation about writing in the academy.

But a safe house requires construction in the writing center. "Safe houses" become safe houses only when tutors realize that they ought not to disinherit their tutees, when they learn not to shuffle students like a deck of cards, when they learn not to act as judge or jury. I could have done more and better work with Trevor. I could have asked him to turn his cultural capital—his knowledge of the product, "the Reebok Pump," into a site for autoethnography. He might have written about his relationship to the consumer culture; he might have written a commercial or a critique of one. I might have asked him to interrogate his leering look at the attractive secretary. I might have asked him why he thought to write about her "silk stocking," and whether she was doing marginalized work, too. I might have asked him to turn his "embarrassing moment" narrative (the story of a job interview that went poorly) into a parody of the workplace in downtown Chicago. Contact zone theory will not only describe the environment where the tutor and tutee meet, it will provide the tutor with a new engagement with the student's text, with another way of reading. The contact zone allows tutors to see the tutorial as a microcosm of the larger academic, institutional scene; the interplay of tutor and student becomes a metaphor for the writing center's relationship to the university. It should allow tutors to negotiate in the political arena of the university, where the writing tutors and writing center directors can become aware of contact zone symmetry, of the power they wield, and more often of the power they lack. Only when tutors recognize the cultural and political implications of the "contact zone" can the tutorial become a really "safe house" for writing instruction.

Works Cited

Bruffee, Kenneth A. 1984. "Peer Tutoring and the 'Conversation of Mankind.'" In *Writing Centers: Theory and Administration*. Ed. Gary A. Olson. Urbana, IL: NCTE, 3–15.

Harris, Muriel. 1992. "Collaboration Is Not Collaboration Is Not Collaboration: Writing Center Tutorials vs. Peer-Response Groups." *College Composition and Communication* 43.3 (October): 369–83.

Jordan, June. 1985. "Nobody Mean More to Me Than You and the Future Life of Willie Jordan." In *On Call: Political Essays*. Boston, MA: South End Press.

Pratt, Mary Louise. 1991. "Arts of the Contact Zone." *Profession '91*: MLA, 1991. 33–40.

North, Stephen M. "Writing Center Research: Testing Our Assumptions." *Writing Centers: Theory and Administration*. Ed. Gary A. Olson. Urbora, IL: NCTE, 24–35.

Wolff, Janice M. Tutor's Log, 1991–92. Unpublished journal.

5 Negotiating the "Subject" of Composition: Writing Centers as Spaces of Productive Possibilities

Stephen Davenport Jukuri
Michigan Technological University

In this chapter I will tell stories of Carla, Li, Dan, and myself to demonstrate that it is often in the writing center—rather than the classroom—where I can see composition's most vexing questions, particularly that of the subject, most clearly. The conventions of classroom pedagogy—class size, grading procedures, and formalized, historically defined relationships of power—often preclude the relationships that would make our many subjectivities visible.

With the following narratives I will step aside from most of the academic debate about the subject to just experience it, to walk around it, muse, and think—to see how it looks when I examine it through my work with writing center students. If "the subject" is, as Lester Faigley says, "the locus of overlapping and competing discourses . . . a temporary stitching together of a series of often contradictory subject positions" (1992, 9), then perhaps the format of this essay is an appropriate one. With tiny strings of theory, I attempt to stitch together a number of writing center stories. The stories contain a multitude of subject positions for a multitude of students, myself included. They are stories that highlight the complex ways in which we are positioned: by the discourse of our pedagogy, by the books we use, by what we know and how we know it, by our definitions of ourselves, and by our social and cultural values, conventions, and experiences.

And yet, as my second story will demonstrate, writing center work is *not necessarily* free of the same relations and conventions that we struggle to change in our classrooms, for we do not check those positions at the door as we might our coat and hat. Instead, perhaps, the writing center is only a space of still unknown possibilities, one that is not yet defined and institutionalized as tightly as the classroom. It is a space in which it is, still, easier to see the subjectivities that come together to produce each of us, easier to see how discourse shapes us as we shape it, and easier to work between those formations to learn

what it means to be a writer, and to write. And the way we often look
into this less-defined space, and give it temporary shape and form, is
through our stories.

What I hope these stories show, ultimately, is that these subjectivities are positions that can contradict, that can work together, that can
lie there, waiting to be discovered, stepped into, rejected, or changed
and negotiated into something new.

Carla

I had known for a long time who Carla was, but I had never officially
"met" her until she signed up with me for a weekly appointment. One
of her daughters graduated from high school with me nine years earlier, and one of her sons was involved in community theater projects that
I had also worked with. And so, when their names would come up in
her conversation, I knew something of the people she was referring to,
and I knew that I could ask her how they were doing from time to time.
I was also familiar with the place where she had once worked as a nurse,
and thus could see more easily why she was frustrated, why she was
back in school. It seemed Carla had come to the university to open up
new possibilities in her life, including, perhaps, a new line of work.

As the term progressed, I was not only coaching Carla in the writing center, but unlike my work with most students, I also became her
"teacher." She had taken classes in composition twenty years ago, and
had been granted transfer credit for them, but discovered during the
previous term that she had completely lost touch with academic writing. So I had her doing the same things that my own classroom students were doing—reading essays from the "Work" chapter of *Reading
Culture*, working out a definition of "meaningful work," and writing
to communicate their new understanding. I often talked to her about
what had happened in my class, at times just to reassure her—as best
I could tell from my position as teacher—that while my students may
have been younger, they were struggling just as much, asking the same
questions, and sometimes appearing much less engaged than she was.
Insecurity was a definite issue, I realized, as she told me that she had
dropped her first computer-intensive course because she spent the
entire first class period just trying to figure out what a "mouse" was,
when she should have been using it to follow along with her instructor. I reassured her that I could help her learn to use the computer too,
when she was in a position to need it again.

Coaching her, it was hard at times to keep the conversation focused
on the writing rather than the small-town talk that would come so

naturally to the two of us. A mutual friend had asked me to ask her if she knew so-and-so at her place of employment, but I kept putting it off as one more tangent that we couldn't afford to take. Once, I almost mentioned that I knew her neighborhood a little, because I know the woman who lives next door to her. But I stopped myself short, remembering that the woman is the grandmother of my "significant other," another man, and while I thought that Carla could probably "handle it" despite her devout Catholicism, it didn't seem like a good time to take the chance that she might put "it" all together, and then take even more time to negotiate what that would mean to each of us and our work together.

Sometimes, I noticed, it seemed important that I actually say, "As your teacher, I want you to know this . . ." or "As your writing coach, I'm wondering what you think about . . ." And so I did.

We worked well together, I thought, and I could see changes in her writing. But Carla had to leave for Florida halfway through the term, to care for an aunt who had raised her, who eventually died. And I didn't see her again that term.

Considering the Subjectivities Awakened with Carla

Carla: mother of old friends, nurse, dissatisfied professional, insecure returning student, mouse-ignorant dropout, neighbor, Catholic woman, responsive niece. Stephen: friend of children, knowledgeable resident of the same town, coach, teacher, partially out/partially closeted gay man, ex-Catholic, and, ultimately, abandoned for a higher-priority relationship. The array of positions can be startling, and with new ones appearing all the time in our discourse, the connections—and our need to negotiate them—seemed endless. For while the "friend of children" and "local resident" parts of me liked to come out from time to time and talk, the "coach" and "teacher" parts constantly reminded me that we had only one hour a week to work. And while the "partially out gay man" is so only because he has learned to talk freely about his connection to the "grandmother/neighbor," the "coach" preferred to save that information for when it might be more carefully articulated to the "student's" intellectual development. And the "teacher" believed that sexuality need not be made the subject of the discourse at all, being used to, and more comfortable with, keeping the "partially closeted" identity intact for the classroom.

But while the "ex-Catholic" reminds all the other subjectivities of the possible ways the "devout Catholic" might react to a more Catholic approach to sexual expression, those subjectivities argue back that the

"nurse," the "student," and the "mother" would have more open ways
to understand it. Meanwhile, the "dissatisfied professional" seemed to
find the topic of meaningful work appealing, and the "coach" and
"teacher" both enjoyed the interest that she demonstrated. And while
the "local resident" always seemed to struggle to the surface with the
latest gossip, the "returning student" countered with a firm belief that
instead she really had better concentrate on what the "teacher" and
"coach" could offer about academic discourse. Yet, ultimately, the
"responsive niece" took charge and overruled the others, leaving the
"coach" with an empty time slot on the schedule board of the institution, a slot that would eventually be filled by some other "student."

I began with my story of Carla because I think it offers the most clear
and obvious of the multitude of positions that emerge through writing
center relationships, positions affecting how we understood each other,
what we said and when we said it, and how we positioned one another.
And yet, as I continue this essay by briefly examining two of the positions I juggled throughout that relationship—those of coach and
teacher—I can see that the same must be true of classroom learning.
But somehow writing center relationships allow the complexity of the
subject to surface and become more visible.

Using the story of Carla for comparison, I am often struck by the differences between the stories that I tell of teaching first-year composition and the stories I tell of my work as a writing center coach. As a
teacher, I am positioned to talk about the "interesting things" that
somehow happened in class: the surprisingly insightful comments
made by one student who didn't appear to be listening, the unique
experiences that a group uses to explain a theoretical concept to the rest
of the class, the question—asked by another student—that, for
unknown reasons, half of the class seem to recognize as racist while the
other half nod their heads in agreement. As a teacher, I might babble
on and on about the fascinating paper that blossomed out of what had
first seemed a very old and tired argument, and I often lament yet
another "great potential paper" that strangely enough never realized
itself. As a teacher I tell also of the theories that might explain where
my students' work comes from; I confess my uncertainties over how
much of their learning really was related to my teaching, and I talk of
my struggles not only to understand what they say and write but to
figure out how to respond to those writings. As a teacher, I almost
always feel like I don't *really* know what is going on with my students.

But when I compare those stories with the ones I tell as a coach, stories in which I often know where a student's insight came from, in
which I might learn why a student has reacted so negatively to an

instructor's comment, in which I have drawn upon some part of me to establish a connection with some part of them, then I understand the differences between the classroom and the writing center. The stories I tell as a teacher actually sound like stories about how little my students and I know and understand one another. I see little of the actual work it takes to construct a piece of writing (even a process-based classroom brings little more than the intermediate reifications of that process to the surface), I see little of what it means for them to construct their texts, and I share very little of what that same process means for me.

And so, as I tell my subsequent writing center stories, and while they often raise their own difficult questions and concerns, I want to demonstrate that they are stories of social context, relationships, and the negotiation of subject positions that come together for the production of meaning. It is in my stories from the center that I can begin to understand Faigley's most vexed question of the subject, trying not so much for *answers*, but instead for ways to think through the question, ways to make that question my own.

With this second story, I come to understand how much of our classroom roles my students and I might bring into the center, how strong those roles can be, and how a writing center relationship is not necessarily much different from my most unsatisfying teaching experiences.

Li

Li arrived for his first session; without saying more than "hello," he placed his ESL handbook on the desk and pointed out an exercise that he didn't understand. I explained it as best I could, though I have become more and more intimidated by grammar exercises myself. As a student, I had always considered them easy and formulaic, an easy shot at a good grade; as a teacher, however, I have learned to recognize the enormous complexity that such exercises always hide. But intimidation aside, in the back of my mind I was mostly trying to figure out what class he was in, what his workbook—which I had never seen before—was supposed to be teaching him, and how I might be able to begin some sort of conversation. I decided that he was probably Chinese, but I've never been very good at guessing ethnic identities (typical American, I think to myself, no knowledge of geography or other cultures). Perhaps his ethnic background shouldn't matter, I decided . . . but perhaps it does, because it no doubt plays some part in how he learns and uses language.

His questions were a constant stream, and when we finally got our noses out of that workbook, it was only because our time was up: my next student had arrived. I had yet to learn anything about him, or he about me. And being relatively new to coaching at the time, I was bewildered by the session, feeling as though I didn't even have a *chance* to ask anything: he had made no eye contact, instead keeping his head down, listening for answers as he watched the book, pointing out each new question as soon as I had answered the last one.

This pattern repeated itself throughout the term, in between missed appointments and a couple of late arrivals with five minutes left in our half-hour session. Not sure if more personal questions would be offensive to him, the most I managed was to ask which class he was in and what some of his grammar assignments were. I never knew that he was doing any writing, though I found out at the end of the term, from his instructor, that he had been producing papers all along. Instead, we spent our time on exercises that he took very seriously—and I, fumbling to explain how more than one grammar construction is possible depending upon the intention and context of the sentence, was questioned constantly on matters of correctness . . . by myself as well as by him.

Finally, in the last five minutes of our last session, Li pulled out maps and pictures of his home and showed them to me. We talked about Malaysia a bit, and I asked a few questions to demonstrate that I was sincerely interested. But I had to keep them brief: we were once again running into my next student's time slot. I asked him to come back next term with those materials, hoping that we could talk more about his home and learn more about each other.

Then Li left, and I never saw him again.

Considering Multiple Subjectivities Involved with Li

For insight on this story, I turn to a few words from Michael Holzman's "Teaching Is Remembering" that continue to ring true for me. He tells me that the key to literacy is not only the demystification of the world (instruction as to what things are and how they work—the role most often assigned to teachers), but it is also "our willingness to give up the protection of our roles as teachers, to remember each of them (students) as individuals, to agree that our relationships are personal. Relationships between individuals," he asserts, "must replace relationships between roles" (1984, 235).

Holzman gives me what I need to reflect on my work with Li, to see that I was merely filling the role of teacher, and a particularly narrow and overdetermined one at that. But, at the same time, I felt positioned that way by Li's actions, a performance of his student role that seemed most mechanical. Obviously, we allowed that space of productive possibilities, the writing center, to default into defining us with time constraints, teachers' expectations, and other formalities no different from the typical classroom.

It is no surprise, when I look at how we positioned ourselves and each other as student and teacher, that I was unable to assert any alternative to the question-answer format, the right vs. wrong answers, and the focus on language solely in its most mechanical sense. The only way, in fact, that our session looked any different from a classroom was the interesting reversal of our roles: the student was asking the questions, while the teacher-coach was struggling to provide correct answers. Perhaps that reversal was especially important, because it taught me that I did not like the way that I was positioned. Like so many classroom students, I was uncomfortable. I resisted by trying to show the exceptions to the rules and the effects of context on meaning. As a language-conscious person who had read *Errors and Expectations* several years earlier, I yearned at the very least to place our work on grammar within some kind of "real" writing context, preferably one that would be meaningful to both of us.

But, just as was true when I was a student of grammar myself, I played the game without trying to change it, perhaps not even knowing how to change it. My experience with Li has shown me that to simply empower students to be "in charge" of their education, such as some might say Li exemplified as he exercised his "question-control" over me, changes little else about how we have been positioned. It amounts at best to a role reversal, rather than providing some way for us to change or re-create the relationship into something that the two of us might really want or need.

To the extent to which we carried only the roles of student and teacher into the writing center, and locked out any alternatives, it became equally true that we were limiting our possibilities—I couldn't even ask him if those exercises were helping, if he had any "real" writing to work on, or if there were any other way to work together that might possibly *mean* something to me as well as him.

I would like to argue, though, that what seems particularly valuable about writing center stories is that even stories like that of Li do not remain as isolated as my classroom/teacher stories often do. Whereas students and teachers are often constructed in singular roles, writing center work often allows for a continuous play of multiple constructions for coaches and students that inform one another.

The relationships that are built with *individual* students, as Holzman calls for, are with individuals to the extent to which they are not limited to singular, predetermined roles, but instead recognize how they are multiply constructed. And as those multiple constructions are discovered and experienced, the range of possibilities for other relationships opens up. When I compare my experience with Li to my subsequent work with other students—both international and American—I see that I need not have stayed buried in those exercises, need not have subjected myself to them, or passively accepted the role that "he" (and everything that positioned *him*) created for me. I could have overcome my own shyness and asserted a few questions toward him, I could have learned some of his language, and I even could have explained what was behind my frustrations with the work we were doing. Perhaps, if I had known more about him, and had expressed that interest, he would have come more, been on time more, and have come back for more. At the least, he may have become comfortable with stepping out of his "student" position sooner, and shared his homeland with me before it was too late. But, not really knowing each other—as individuals, in multiple ways, through our multiple subjectivities—made it nearly impossible for anything meaningful to happen, much less for me to understand the relationship in any meaningful way.

As when I teach, with Li I will never feel as though I can believe I actually helped him. In fact, I don't believe I did. And yet, as useful as those little lines from Holzman can be, I still puzzle over what it might mean to have an *individual* relationship, for as should be obvious by now, I am drawn to the poststructuralist and postmodern discussions that have deconstructed notions of both "the individual" and "the subject" as unified and centered entities, claiming instead that individuals are multiply subjected, multiply constructed, and at the same time able to construct and subject themselves in relation to others.

I ask: what becomes of "you," "he," "she," "I," and "us," when the individual "I"s and "you"s begin to look more and more like many different people rolled into one?

To illustrate a relationship that positions students into wholly individualized roles that are unrecognizable to, and not necessarily valued by, any established discourse, I continue with the story of Dan, reconstructed from one entry in my session notes.

Dan

Dan got a paper back from his instructor. The instructor noted that the paper didn't seem to have any "thesis." And so, we went about trying to figure out what "thesis" was, and what that might mean. I questioned him about what he wanted to say about the text he had read (a literary one), what he specifically saw in the text, and what significance it might hold for him. I took a couple pages of dictation from his answers, and I tried to talk through how his statements could be formulated into one or two different theses. But then he said, "But I still don't know why my paper isn't already okay." At that point, I was beginning to wonder the same thing myself. After all, what *was* wrong with the paper? He had constructed it fairly carefully, he had "chosen" to write it that way and to say what he did, and it wasn't even full of errors. But, like papers that are "just my opinion" (as students often say), and papers that are well-crafted but entirely personal expositions, Dan's paper didn't really seem to be trying to mean anything to me.

And so I looked at it again, this time reading it out loud, and I responded with the word "okay" after each paragraph, using a tone of voice intended to signal him that he had simply reported what the text had said in his own words, providing nothing of interest to me, nothing that would cause me to have any response other than "Okay—what's the point?" By the end of page one, he interrupted with, "Okay, I get it now, I'm only talking about the story, and only telling what's in the story, not anything else." "I think that's it," I said, and I explained that, in a sense, he needed to keep the story there as examples and illustrations, but that yes, actually, he also needed to be focused on ideas and concepts in such a way that they might become relevant to something—and somebody else—outside of his own personal experience with the story he read.

Considering Subjectivities with Dan

Do I work with students as though they must be completely other to everyone else? Do I want Dan to simply say anything he wants, which in this case amounted to, ironically, what he had probably been trained to do in past English classes? Do I want him to repeat what he has read in exact and precise terms, with correct grammar and spelling, and without engaging himself or his readers in any intellectual way?

Of course I don't want that, I automatically reply, though I can't ever completely shake off the discourse that calls for freewriting, that asks for affirmations of his authentic voice despite where it comes from and what it says, that reminds me how liberating it once was for me to fill page after page of my very first journal as a senior in high school. But with a paper that had to be revised, and for which I could see good arguments for revision, I was more concerned at the moment with how Dan might be able to "invent the university." I wondered how he might engage with some of the more commonly accepted conventions of academic discourse that would help him to reposition others.

My simple but repeated response—"okay" with a nod of my head to affirm that I easily "got" the info but could really use something more meaningful to me—was enough to show him that he was not really doing anything for anyone else, much less himself, with his paper. He was not attempting to change me, not attempting to change anything about himself, not asking me to struggle for something new.

I worry about both approaches, that I will either be fitting students into over- and predetermined positions, or I will be letting them do and say whatever they want. Either way, I am in constant risk of falling completely into one or the other of the pole positions, for as Kurt Spellmeyer explains in *Common Ground* (1993), such tendencies are inherent in language.

He explains that Michel Foucault, in his "Discourse on Language," refers to two "voices" that parallel my concern and mirror the extremes of my continuum: the first voice, called Institution, offers security and "the safety of roles prepared in advance" (72). The voice of Institution makes me wonder: if I am doing well enough myself, as writing coach, teacher, member of this institution of higher learning, and active citizen, would my students not be best off doing the very same? And do they not often seek that security themselves, asking me how *I* would write the paper, how *I* would make the decisions on how to meet the assignment?

The second voice, which Foucault calls Inclination, "dreams of language without prohibitions, where writers can choose whatever roles they please" (72). It is this voice that tells me it is better to let students speak freely than to restrict their freedom or risk violating their sensibility with conventions of discourse that don't work for them.

But there is a possibility of a third voice, one much more difficult to recognize, to talk about, and to speak with; for, as Spellmeyer points out, the "two misleading speakers, who seduce by telling exactly one-half of the truth, sound so much like ourselves" (72). We talk in terms of institution—fitting ourselves into the roles that the institution defines—and we talk in terms of inclination—expressing ourselves authentically and free of restraints and restrictions—but it is the third voice that I believe we must search for, in ourselves and in our students. It would be a voice that can learn to work between those two extremes, to facilitate a mutual negotiation between the individual and the institution, working with individuals not only to occupy and employ a multitude of subject positions but to gain some control over their construction, to negotiate their terms, to re-create them, and to open up new fields of possibilities for ourselves and each other.

My search for that third voice is, I remind myself, a matter of *constantly* reminding myself: reminding myself that Faigley defines the subject as "the locus of overlapping and competing discourses . . . a temporary stitching together of a series of often contradictory subject positions" (1992, 9). And so I remind myself that at any one moment Carla is holding together her life as a nurse, mother, returning student, responsible relative, disgruntled worker, devout Catholic, and neighbor: never able to be all at once, but instead working always from some configuration of them even as she tries to develop one or another of those positions. I remind myself, from Michael Holzman, that literacy and learning require a *relationship* between individuals. I remind myself that the particular contexts and subjectivities through which selves are constituted are going to be, more often than not, different. And I remind myself to work with Dan to show him some conventions of academic discourse, and to create a more specific subject position that might allow him to express himself in ways that his particular academic audience will be interested in reading.

I realize that it is not *impossible* to make those same reminders in the classroom. As Diana George and Diane Shoos tell us in "Issues of Subjectivity and Resistance" (1992), although a student's theorizing in a final paper may seem inconsistent with previous writings, and may appear to be a lapse into an uncritical subjectivity that clashes with pedagogical goals, we (as teachers) can resist seeing such "affronts" to our own subjectivities as failure by instead looking carefully at what negotiations that student is making. In the case of their particular examination, they demonstrate that one student's description of the pleasurable experience of game shows is not necessarily incompatible with the student's critical understanding of the way in which those shows position and construct individuals—the student included—throughout our society.

George and Shoos tell us that we "need to remind ourselves of the often hidden complexity of students' work," we must "be attentive to the possibility that (their) discourse inscribes a multiple rather than centered subjectivity," and that it is equally important to understand "our own position as subject in relation to these texts"—which in their case consists of demonstrating an awareness of the negative ways in which they themselves have experienced and understood game shows, positions that could easily lead them to disregard any "positive" discussion of game shows as being "uncritical" (206). Ultimately, they tell us, we must "run the risk that students will attack the things we love or embrace the things we hate" (209). The challenge is to be able to construct some mutual understanding of how that could be.

So it is possible to remind my selves that my work with students is a matter of relationships between multiple subject positions. And yet it is so very difficult; those subjectivities are, as George and Shoos have said, "often hidden" from me as a teacher, and, as Faigley says, "the notion of subjectivity itself . . . is far too complex to be 'read off' from texts"; subject positions are momentary, partial, temporary, and occupied with different degrees of investment (110). As a teacher who must work with many individuals all at once, who knows students mostly through their texts, I often find it nearly impossible to *experience* those subjectivities and their positions in the classroom; I usually cannot discern some third voice whispering somewhere in between institutions and inclination. Instead, to find that voice, I return to the stories that I tell of my work at the writing center, work that I attempt to construct within the range of what I consider to be the real question: Do I work with students such that we might negotiate our subjectivities within a context of mutual learning, sharing of experience, collaborative construction of text, and the production of knowledge?

Dan, Revisited

I didn't mention earlier that Dan used to be the work-study assistant in the writing center, a position he lost due to poor grades. As part of his plan to stay in school, he signed up with one writing coach for time management and study skills, and was working with me on his writing class. As the term progressed, I discovered that Dan often didn't seem interested in talking much about "writing"—maybe he just wasn't yet able to, or didn't have the vocabulary—and subsequently I found myself becoming more directive and "instructive" with him, giving him specific strategies to try for revision. But during our eighth session (out of nine), I finally asked him some questions that resulted in, I think, a more collaborative learning experience, one that may have made more sense to him than anything I had said or done earlier. The session had begun in an "instructive" mode: he had a draft, and asked for some response on it. As I read, I explained some of the confusion that I experienced, and connected those particular experiences with explanations of what my expectations are for the genre of academic writing. I asked if he knew what "genre" meant; he wasn't sure, and so I explained it in terms of how academic writing is different from other "kinds"—other "genres"— of writing, such as mystery stories and novels, and I included reasons why those differences are important to readers and writers. He responded by telling me that he really doesn't like to get into the kinds of details that academic writing requires.

So I leaned back a bit in my chair, and asked if he had found an area of study yet in which he enjoyed getting into the details and particulars. It turned out he does like writing computer programs, and he was thinking about choosing computer science for his major. And fortunately again, my brief search for some subject other than writing, some subject position other than "essay writer," led into a conversation about the ways in which writing computer programs is similar to writing papers. Good programs, we decided, have clear comment lines that explain to other programmers what the program is trying to accomplish and how it is accomplishing it, just like academic papers often have "comment" statements, directives as to what readers should expect, and elaborations on how they should read and understand examples. Good programs have procedures and subroutines that are in many ways separate from the main program, but still must fit with it, and are all very important to the overall functioning of the program as a whole, just like academic papers have separate illustrations, examples, and points that all function somewhat independently, but are connected by the ways they work together to create a better understanding of the writer's argument.

For ten minutes, I remembered what it was once like to be a computer science major myself, a role that I had given up seven years earlier: the excitement of creating programs that would work, that could solve problems, that would ultimately be useful and meaningful to others. But back then, my grades only told me that I knew how to write A programs as well as A papers—not until I worked with Dan did I begin to understood how much the two were all alike and what they had in common. And how it was that I could be so interested in both.

Reconsidering Dan

Whether or not those sessions with Dan were "successful" is hard to know for sure; in the writing center, unlike the classroom, definitions of success are often a function of the relationships established, not tied so strongly to any particular measure of one person's work against another's. Those sessions felt successful *to me* because I knew at least that I had learned something, and I felt that we had effectively negotiated at least one subject position (for Dan, that of computer programmer) with a position that was unfamiliar, one that he was struggling with, one that he needed some access to: that of academic writer.

While it may have been serendipitous that I had once defined myself as a computer science major, it was not accidental that I sought out those connections, asking him more about who he was, sharing who I was, learning what he identified with, and who he wanted to be: a computer programmer. As a programmer he might actually have learned from me something more valuable to him about computer programming than about writing.

To find meaningful connections and common ground, to begin to intersect our multiple subject positions with one another, we had to discover what directions the conversation *could* take, allow other subjectivities to come in and inform our discussions, and make choices about which ones might lead to productive work.

Often I can work with what we lay out on the table; sometimes I can't.

In fact, if one wonders why I do not seem to bring up my sexuality with students, I would respond that it is because I so rarely find a way to do it that I believe would be productive. Instead, it comes up more often outside of the writing center, and beyond the classroom, when my pedagogical relationship with a student carries on beyond those contexts and changes into a relationship in which bringing out that part of myself is somehow important to the development of our thinking, our ability to work together, our friendship, or our politics. In other words, the forces that define the context of those two institutional roles, as well as the greater social forces that articulate sexuality into very particular and singular roles, all make it less likely that my articulation of myself as a gay man would be useful or acceptable in my educational relationships. Yet I am open to that possibility as much as any other, and I am more likely to find it in the writing center than in the classroom.

And it is because I see the writing center as a place for opening up productive possibilities, and the classroom, too often, used as a place for restricting and channeling productive activities in particular ways, that I believe it is important to note that in coaching I learn what it means to resist trying to know, ahead of time, what will happen when I explore the subjective positions I occupy. Questions that open up productive possibilities are important, Spellmeyer tells us, because they are what he calls, in terms of learning, "real questions": "those for which the teacher (does) not already have an answer" (1993, 136). George and Shoos echo the need for such uncertainty in education, asserting that "the healthiest critique occurs when everyone involved—instructor as well as students—has yet to take a set position on a text" (1992, 207). This allows dialogue that includes and creates an understanding of the multiple ways that people are positioned in their lives, and how they will bring those subjectivities to bear upon the work at hand. And finally, when Foucault reflects on his own intellectual development, he tells us that the result of such uncertain explorations can turn us into something new, render us no longer the same and no longer able to see ourselves and others in the same way ("The 'Experience-Book'" 1991). Referring to his books as "experiences," he explains that "an experience is something you come out of changed. If I had to write a book to communicate what I have already thought, I'd never have the courage to begin it. I write precisely because I don't know yet what to think about a subject that attracts my interest. In so doing, the book transforms me, changes what I think" (27).

Likewise, by not determining answers ahead of time, it is possible to realize, re-create, negotiate, and reconfigure the multitude of subject positions that constitute teachers and students. And while neither my students nor I tend to *radically* transform ourselves, it is true that as we work together, we do change, we do discover differences, and we do begin to see what it means to resurrect old subject positions, to learn new ones, to act differently within them, to shape ourselves into something a little bit other than what we were before. We often change the way we think, and we often change the way we write as well.

Yet, I remind myself how difficult that can be: there are times when I listen to myself and I hear the voice of the institution, finding it easier to see difference as failure, than to see difference as an opportunity to engage with, and learn from, the individual who constitutes that difference out of a multitude of equally valid discourses. There are times when I hear the voice of inclination, articulating difference as mere difference rather than engaging with it, and the student who exemplifies it, to construct the common ground between us that might lead to respect, learning, and something worth writing about.

Finally, as a teacher, it is difficult to be changed by my students when my grades and my work and my evaluations have continually told me that I myself have been a successful student of writing. From that subject position I am often too quick to recognize what would work for *me*, and too slow to see and understand how something *else* might work better for the *writer*. I am too different from them, sometimes, to know where to begin, or how to ask.

But I also remind myself of how Anne DiPardo characterized writing center tutors in "Whispers of Coming and Going." Much like students, she says, tutors "occupy multiple roles, remaining learners even while emerging as teachers, perennially searching for a suitable social stance (Hawkins)—a stance existing somewhere along a continuum of detached toughness and warm empathy" (1992, 125–26). And I strive for what she lays out in her conclusion: that individuals who work in writing centers must be "respectfully curious" about their students, must have practical strategies that are informed by theory, and must have compelling reminders of the need to monitor themselves. "Most of all, we must serve as models of reflective practice—perennially inquisitive and self-critical, even as we find occasion both to bless and curse the discovery that becoming students of students means becoming students of ourselves as well" (142).

It is easy to *believe*, as a teacher as well as a coach, that I must be a learner of my students, for by positioning them to be my teachers I allow them to see themselves as people who have experience, who can produce knowledge, and who can construct meaningful text for others. It is easy to believe, as a coach as well as a teacher, that I still need to do some amount of "teacher talk," providing students with knowledge, information, strategies, and theoretical models. And it is easy to *believe*, for both myself and my students, that our learning depends upon developing our awareness of our multiple subjectivities, communicating them, and allowing ourselves the opportunities to discover, create, and practice various positions in order to learn how to negotiate them. And of course, I *know* that I need to affirm and value their individual experiences and contributions that grow out of those multiple subjectivities.

But as a writing coach, I have learned that in the writing center I am in a better position to *experience* what I believe. There I am in a very unique position, one in which I often have just enough time and space to listen to them as individuals, to learn what they have to communicate, and to see what it will take to construct points of negotiation between their lives and the positions, experiences, and discourses. What I learn in the writing center informs the way I construct my role as classroom teacher, but it is as a writing coach that I can really listen to myself and my students, remember the stories we tell, and recognize not only the ways in which we construct those narratives, but also how we come to construct each other within them.

Carla Revisited

Five months later, Carla returned and we dug back into composition, this time our efforts split between writing a paper for me and her work for an introductory class in scientific and technical communication. For me, she read about rap music, experienced a particular approach to cultural analysis, and took on new strategies for conducting research, producing knowledge, and constructing text. As her work progressed, she told me how she suddenly noticed that her sixteen-year-old son listens to rap, and she talked to him about it, trying to make sense of the readings she had to respond to. She discussed rap with her husband, and they began to see it everywhere: TV, magazines, newspapers. He showed her an article by a woman her age who came to understand that rap really is music, and the article became central to the argument she developed in her paper. And while she was still offended by rap lyrics, and says she always will be, she was able to realize things she had not understood before, and she wrote her paper to communicate her new understanding to others.

But as we moved along through the term, we also talked of other things—her family, the choir that she was singing in (for which my significant other was the assistant conductor), a lot about nursing and taking care of patients, and of course her other class. And, eventually, she had to write a "reading response" on how Aristotle defines the difference between art and science. She struggled, not only with the suggested questions but also with her confidence and perceived ability to attempt any interpretation at all. So I asked her: do you see nursing as a science or an art? And she told me that it is both; that it is a science because there are so many set procedures for everything, and specific steps to follow, and ways to assure that you can "prove" the accuracy of your work—some of which is part of what she has come to hate about the job. And yet it is an art, because she works with people, people who don't always fit the procedures, people who require creative solutions. She told me how she had to develop a new way to secure an IV for a patient who kept loosening it. And she told me, more importantly perhaps, that when she questioned the man's wife about why they had not answered their phone earlier in the day, she "pretended not to hear" the woman apologize and "confess" that, against doctor's orders, they had gone for a ride in the car because he wanted so badly to be outside. She understood that he was more than just a patient, and had more needs than just those that the doctor might order.

And after we had written down all that she had said, and we looked it over, she glanced back at the assignment, frowned, and worried out loud that she hadn't answered the questions the way she thought she was supposed to. But, just as quickly, she changed her expression and told me that while she might not have answered the question exactly, she thinks that's okay, because she's not only starting to understand this science vs. art stuff from Aristotle, but also has realized that it's okay to talk about her own experience in this thing called a reading response.

Carla, One Year Later

As we looked at her papers and discussed her course in communication theory, Carla talked on and on about how she couldn't believe that there could be so many different theories for one thing—before this class, as far as she was concerned people just talked to one another. For her final paper, she wrote about how rhetorical theories of communication can explain not only how her favorite author, Leo Buscaglia, writes, but also how doctor-patient communication often fails when doctors overestimate the power of their ethos and address only the logos of their patients' problems. We used one session just to talk about how she was planning her degree, and she explained that she had decided that she wanted to continue nursing, but figured she could add variety for herself by doing technical communication projects for the home nursing company she works for. So we looked through the catalogue to find courses that would help her reach that goal and fit into her degree schedule as well, and she decided that the document design class offered next winter would be useful. We made plans to learn the computer software for that class ahead of time, trying to be sure that she would be positioned for success.

At the end of the term, she was taking private voice lessons from my significant other, and often gave me messages to pass on to him. I began to think that maybe she had recognized what position we were in, and that maybe it would soon be time to begin talking about it more explicitly.

Acknowledgments

There are a number of people who have worked very hard to make my subject "position" both comfortable and possible. They include Nancy Grimm, Dennis Lynch, Diana George, Daniel Hendrickson, and the many other colleagues and students with whom I continually feel privileged to work.

Works Cited

DiPardo, Anne. 1992. "'Whispers of Coming and Going': Lessons from Fannie." *Writing Center Journal* 12.2 (Spring): 125–44.

Faigley, Lester. 1992. *Fragments of Rationality: Postmodernity and the Subject of Composition*. Pittsburgh: University of Pittsburgh Press.

Foucault, Michel. 1991. Interview. "The 'Experience-Book.'" *Remarks on Marx: Conversations with Duccio Trombadori*. Trans. James Goldstein and James Cascaito. New York: Semiotext(e).

George, Diana, and Diane Shoos. 1992. "Issues of Subjectivity and Resistance: Cultural Studies in the Composition Classroom." In *Cultural Studies in the*

English Classroom. Eds. James A. Berlin and Michael J. Vivion. Portsmouth, NH: Boynton/Cook, Heinemann, 200–10.

Holzman, Michael. 1984. "Teaching Is Remembering." *College English* 46.3 (March): 229–38.

Spellmeyer, Kurt. 1993. *Common Ground: Dialogue, Understanding, and the Teaching of Composition.* Upper Saddle River, NJ: Prentice Hall.

6 Disruptions, Differences, and Bakhtin's Dialogic

Laura Rogers
Albany College of Pharmacy

Carolyn A. Statler
Albany College of Pharmacy

Mary and one of her friends sat uncomfortably and silently at the writing center table. On the table between us was Mary's paper, a graphic account of sexual abuse, written in response to a personal experience essay assignment. I had sent her a note asking her to stop by, but I wasn't sure what I was going to say to her. She wasn't quite sure why she was at the writing center.

Jim's response to this assignment (and to subsequent ones) was to write a lengthy, violent "Dungeons and Dragons" type story. What sort of response was this to a class writing assignment? What possible response could we make to this paper?

Linda sat stiffly in the chair across from me while tears of anger, frustration, and embarrassment ran down her face, the obviously plagiarized paper, free of the deviations from convention that characterized all her other papers, between us. I attempted again to explain to her that she could not turn this paper in; she again tearfully insisted that "at my other school, this was how I always wrote my papers."

As we thought about student writing at our school, we felt that our students, for the most part, produce safe, predictable papers that offer pat answers to truly complex questions such as "What is something that has changed your life?" or to philosophical struggles with assigned texts. The papers are reasonably "well written" in grammatical terms, but often the writers do not seem truly engaged. At times, however, papers such as these grabbed everyone's attention, disrupting our world of safe, predictable papers. We began to see these disruptions as instances where students were truly engaged. They had crossed discursive boundaries; they came up against perceived limitations of traditional definitions of school writing or invoked social and cultural contexts that likewise violated the boundaries of academic discourse.

We have returned to these stories again and again because we were not happy with our roles and our responses. What could we have done differently and why did our responses feel so "not right?" There are other stories that are equally troubling, instances when we were happy with our responses; we had had interesting and thoughtful conversations with students. However, to our dismay, the papers written subsequent to those conversations were "safe and predictable" and showed little or no evidence that the conversation had ever occurred.

Diane, for example, struggled with issues of racism in her own life as we talked about how she might respond to Martin Luther King's "Letter from Birmingham Jail." During our writing conference, she raised many difficult and disturbing questions as she tried to explore racism in her own community and in her own experience. Her final draft, however, did not include that exploration. I did not question her about why she had chosen to evade the tough, complex questions we had discussed earlier.

The stories we have recounted are not the only disruptions that occurred, but they are ones in which our responses made us uncomfortable; we searched for a means of rethinking our roles as writing center instructors and the circumstances of student writing at our institution. This search led, finally, to the work of Russian rhetorician Mikhail Bakhtin and to an article by C. H. Knoblauch, "Rhetorical Constructions: Dialogue and Commitment" (1988), in which Knoblauch draws on Bakhtin's work and brings it closer to our immediate concerns. We believed that we could use Bakhtin's and Knoblauch's theories about the social nature of language as lenses with which to reexamine and to reimagine these stories. Could we read these stories as truly telling utterances of Bakhtin's "clown, fool and rogue" as students tried to engage in what we understand Bakhtin to mean as "authentic discourse"?

Both Bakhtin and Knoblauch see language as social and always contextual and conditional. Bakhtin identifies the site of language as "heteroglossia," all the conditions which ensure that "at any given time, at any given place, there will be a set of conditions—social, historical, meterological, physiological that will ensure that a word uttered in that place and at that time will have a meaning different than it would have under any other conditions" (Holquist, in Bakhtin 1981, 428). Heteroglossia ensures the primacy of context over text. It is exciting to think in terms of the uniqueness of writing and conversations in this place and at this time, and Bakhtin allows us to see the unique nature of our institution, the place of writing, and the writing center as important pieces of why these disruptions occurred, and why we responded as we did.

Our writing center is located in a small college of pharmacy. The life of the college is influenced by the fact that everyone is pursuing the same degree (although not necessarily the same career) and that there is nearly a 100 percent placement rate after graduation at very high entry-level salaries. When we first arrived here, students were described to us as placid; they were polite, we were told, and wouldn't give us any trouble, but we should not expect particularly strong writing from them.

Although the curricular focus in this school is on the sciences, students are required to take thirty hours of humanities. Curricular restructuring in 1986 created interdisciplinary, primarily freshman-level humanities courses and eliminated the traditional freshman composition course. The writing center was established, on the advice of an outside consultant, to serve the need for "good" writing. Theoretically, the writing center is to serve the entire college, but we believe we are generally seen as part of the liberal arts department, and we see mostly students from the first-year "Humanities Preceptorial" classes.

As our positions were originally constructed, the tasks of the writing center were to work with individuals or small groups of students on writing assignments, conduct writing workshops in the humanities classes, and most uniquely to act as "readers" of freshman papers before the individual faculty read and responded to them. Students turned in papers to their professors who, in turn, brought the essays to the writing center before reading and responding to them. The essays (which students only wrote one draft of) were then "corrected," in the most traditional sense of the word, by the writing center instructors. We were to respond only to sentence-level error; "content" was exclusively the province of the professor.

Our primary functions, then, seemed to be constructed as helping students with their papers and serving as "paper correctors," comma fixers, and error finders for faculty. In our office, there were file drawers filled with worksheets on grammar, diagnostic skills tests, and computer-assisted grammar programs. We also found that faculty were particularly concerned about error in the writing of students for whom English is a second language, although no formal classes or support systems exist to meet their needs.

The institution does not offer support for students for whom English is a second language, yet most of the faculty here require immediate adherence to conventions of written and spoken English. This school believes itself to be a "quiet" place free of racial and gender tensions that have caused disruption and conflict on so many college campuses. At this school, there is no Educational Opportunity Program, no Affirmative Action office, no office of Minority Student Affairs, no women's groups or gay and lesbian organizations. The school is officially "silent" about all of these troubling matters.

This institution, of course, is not free from these kinds of tensions; racial and gender differences exist here as they do everywhere, as evidenced by students like Mary and other women who have told similar stories of date rape and stalking, by students who have told stories about racial conflict, and by students who have come to the writing center and cried over problems they defined as racial.

Although both of us were troubled by the definition of the writing center's position and the school's description of students and representation of itself, and although we both came from backgrounds in which discourse is conceived of very differently than it is here, we accepted the positions as they were structured because our part-time status met our own economic and personal needs. We were both in the process of working on our dissertations and one of us had two small children. We both believed that we would be in this position for a short time; we saw our place here as "temporary." Once here, however, we found that we could not live comfortably within the parameters defined for us. We were far more concerned with what students were thinking and writing than with grammatical error.

To be fair, things have changed since we began working in the writing center. In some classes, students are asked to write more than one draft of papers and our response to student papers for their instructors now takes a much more holistic form, although we sometimes find ourselves responding to error more than we feel comfortable with. We have cleaned out the filing cabinet.

As we read Bakhtin's work, we began to think about language in his terms and to realize some reasons for our discomfort with our original tasks. For Bakhtin, the basic unit of language is not the sentence or the word, any grammatical or semantic unit, but the utterance, defined as speech whose natural boundary is the speech of the other, which constitutes a dialogue. Utterances can be of any length, from a single word to a multivolume work. Each utterance is filled with "echoes and reverberations" of other utterances to which it is related and invites a response from the addressee (a particular individual or even a whole culture). "The utterance is filled with dialogic overtones. After all, our thought itself—philosophical, scientific, artistic—is born and shaped in the process of interaction and struggle with other thoughts" (Bakhtin 1986b, 92).

We were asked initially to address sentence-level error in student writing; we were to concern ourselves with a grammatical unit which, because it lacks expressiveness, is different from an utterance. We wanted to be and were responders to student "utterances," the meaning of their texts, because to do otherwise was a philosophical anathema and because writing centers, by their nature, are places where dialogue occurs.

For Bakhtin, dialogue is the natural state; monologue is virtually impossible because there is always some response. Even silence or failure to respond is a response. In one of the few places where Bakhtin mentions education directly, he says that education tends to be a monologic rather than a dialogic activity. That has appeared to be true at our school. Students are asked to produce written material in response to other writers or even in response to their own lives, but that material is turned in for evaluation rather than eliciting responses that even hint at the heteroglossia governing the teacher's response or the student's writing. According to Bakhtin, dialogism is the "characteristic epistemological mode of a world dominated by heteroglossia. Everything means, is understood as part of a greater whole—there is a constant interaction between meanings, all of which have the potential of conditioning others" (Holquist, in Bakhtin 1981, 428). This "constant interaction between meanings" is important and enriching.

We have found it useful and helpful in rereading these "disruptive" instances in the writing center to understand that there are, according to Bakhtin, centripetal, centralizing forces in any language or culture which exercise a "homogenizing and hierarchizing" influence. Opposed to these are centrifugal forces creating alternative "degraded" genres. In *Discourse in the Novel*, Bakhtin identifies these centrifugal forces as the "clown, the rogue and the fool." According to Bakhtin, because there is no possible "straightforward truth," the centrifugal, dispersing forces of the clown, rogue and fool are opposed to "offical" language that pretends to be monologic (Discourse 401–2). We are appropriating these terms, not as novelistic devices, but as disruptive forces in the life of the writing center and this institution.

In the stories with which we began, there appear characters who appear to be "clowns, fools or rogues," writers who disregarded the rules of academic discourse at this school. Mary shared an intensely private part of her life and her explicit discussion of a sexual experience unsettled us all. Jim, the "science fiction writer," disregarded (or so we thought at the time) the instructor's assignment and turned in an "off-the-wall" response that we could not make heads or tails of. Linda disturbed us because plagiarism is always a disruption in the academy, a flagrant disregard of the protocol of academic society. With her discussion of racial issues, Diane was moving beyond the needs of the assignment into territory that may have felt scary to anyone, particularly at an institution with no public forums for discussing difficult issues. She chose ultimately to align herself with centripetal forces.

In our responses to these "disruptions," because the roles the students chose were so far outside their usual academic subjectivities, we could not decide who we were. Were we part of the centripetal, hierarchizing forces, or were we clowns, fools, or rogues? In our choices, we tried to straddle the fence and attempted to support both centripetal and centrifugal forces. When centrifugal forces produced a most disquieting effect, as in Mary's case, we sought guidance from our director and other professors. All of us were honestly concerned; all of us felt helpless; all of us wished, at some level, that these writers had not disturbed us. On the other hand, we felt equally uneasy about writers who finally chose not to invoke what they knew from their own lives and experiences.

Even without the work of Bakhtin and Knoblauch, we have been steadily moving to a dialogic approach to writing and learning. We were first drawn to social constructionism, but that view seemed incomplete. While that approach is concerned with the social nature of language, Bakhtin and Knoblauch move beyond that to ethical questions as well. We began to see the importance of our "response" both in terms of responding to students and student texts and in terms of our *responsibility* to students and their work. And it is in that issue of responsibility that we face our most difficult questions.

Because we were not happy with our responses and felt we had been neither "responsible" nor "answerable," both in our literal responses to students and in terms of responsible, ethical actions, Bakhtin's use and definition of the term "answerability" are important to us. In his short essay "Art and Answerability," Bakhtin discusses the separation of art and life when the artist and the human being are united "mechanically" in one person and are not "imbued with internal unity of meaning" (1990, 1). What guarantees that unity of the constituent elements of a person is "Only the unity of answerability. I have to answer with my own life for what I have experienced and understood in art, so that everything I have experienced and understood would not remain ineffectual in my life" (1). However, the concept of answerability also entails mutual liability to blame and an emphasis on individual accountability (Ewald 1993, 340).

As we thought about these troubling, "disruptive" stories and tried to imagine a more "Bakhtinian" kind of response that might truly invite a dialogue, acknowledging and identifying the contextual framework in which we all exist, we believed we could use Knoblauch's ideas about the dialogical nature of language to help us reimagine these stories. In his article, in which Knoblauch defines language as a material and historical act (1988, 134) and argues for a dialogic conception of discourse, he writes that "The ultimate motive for any transformation is, according to Freire, the need to be more fully human, the need to participate more completely and more freely in the world" (125).

Mary and Laura

One of the most compelling narratives, one we keep returning to, invokes a context that in this institution is usually silenced and speaks to the "double message" the institution sends by inviting the personal while at the same time wishing to keep its hands clean of messy personal matters. I had come across Mary's paper in a stack of "personal experience" essays that had been sent to us to "correct." We were shocked by Mary's graphic description of sexual abuse. We wanted to make a personal response that would include a practical, concrete answer to her call for help, offer her a referral to counseling, the phone number of the local rape crisis center. Would these actions be under our jurisdiction, within our authority, we wondered. (This is something we always worry about, as our institutional roles are simultaneously varied and unclear.)

Before we took any of these actions, we felt we needed to check with our director; he referred us to her professor. Both the professor and our director exclaimed, "But this girl seems so happy!" Was it possible she was "making this up," they wondered.

Because her paper was so explicit and so unexpected, doubts were raised about her emotional stability. We were all uncomfortable, not because we weren't all aware of occurrences of rape in our society but because Mary had invoked that social context in an intensely personal way, right in our midst.

We still believe we did the "right," the "answerable" thing in asking Mary to stop by and talk with us, to offer her practical help, to show her that we responded to her utterance with genuine concern and feeling. What we now feel was "not right" was our compliance in a system that does not want to hear about violence between men and women by first checking with our director and her teacher before we responded to her in any way, and our participation in the definition of her as someone who had mistakenly, foolishly written about what should have remained a private issue, someone who might be "crazy," who needed to have her "file checked." As we look back at this incident now, we believe we should have responded directly to Mary's needs rather than seeking "permission" from the institutional authority structures.

A Bakhtinian Reimagining of Mary's Story

We can reread Mary's story through a "Bakhtinian" lens; for example, instead of seeing Mary as someone with a problem who had to be helped in private, we could see her as a Bakhtinian "rogue" or "clown," a border crosser who had explicitly invoked a taboo subject and foregrounded an important social issue. In fact, when Mary first came to the writing center in response to our note, she said that it had been empowering to her to write this paper, had made her feel good; writing this paper, she said, had allowed her to begin to talk to her roommate about her problem and had enabled her to begin to deal with the abusive situation she found herself in.

Instead of foregrounding the empowering nature of Mary's text, encouraging the "roguish" nature of what she had done, we concentrated on Mary as a person with a problem, someone who had to be helped. Had we defined Mary as a Bakhtinian "clown" or "rogue," we could have, for example, applauded her courage in facing and coming to grips with a painful part of her life, for daring to speak about these issues in a public forum, for articulating issues that all women potentially face; her paper might have (without calling attention to Mary) called attention to the social issues of redrawing male/female relationships and the real and prevalent problems of sexual abuse and harassment. We would like to think that we might even have explored with her why the institution has defined her story as "unacceptable" and what that might mean in her life.

And yet, Mary's story called up all the possible voices, the heteroglossia of her utterance; everyone involved had something to say. Bakhtin tells us that the word truly lives only in dialogue, that it "wants to be heard, understood and 'answered' by other voices from other positions" (as quoted in Stewart 1986, 47). Perhaps much of our discomfort arises from the fact that although many voices were sounding, they were not speaking to each other; no new meaning was created. Each new speaker (except, perhaps, for Mary) remained within his or her own world.

Linda and Laura

Linda held back tears.

"What are books for if not to use information from?" she exclaimed, defending once again the clearly plagiarized art history paper. "This has always been the way I have worked."

I did not want Linda to turn this paper in. She was a third-year transfer student, already struggling academically. The essay was so clearly not her work. The papers she wrote for this class had all been returned to her covered with many circles and marks; she wanted badly to do better. The teacher had "suggested" to Linda that she "spend time" in the writing center each week to "improve her English."

I suggested to Linda that we take the paper to the instructor for her response. Linda refused to speak to the instructor but agreed to let me talk to the teacher about the essay myself. Linda cried even harder when I talked to her about the paper again and accused me of calling her a cheat and a liar. When her tears subsided, I tried to work with her on brainstorming ideas for a draft, but she ended up with very few words on paper. The essay she turned in to the instructor was not much different from the initial, plagiarized paper.

A Bakhtinian Reimagining of Linda's Story

In this case of plagiarism and in other similar cases, we and others responded to the grammatical, the string of sentences, rather than the speaker and the utterance. Bakhtin states that ". . . as an utterance (or part of an utterance) no one sentence even if it is only one word, can ever be repeated; it is always a new utterance (even if it is a quotation)" (Speech 108). This is not a defense of plagiarism, an academic offense that can cost an individual her academic career. However, Bakhtin's privileging of the utterance might help us concentrate on the student rather than on the transgression. How might we help the student produce new speech to respond to a text rather than misappropriating it? Could I have talked more with Linda about her utterance? What was her text saying? Perhaps students who plagiarize are trying to commit fraud, to fool the authorities, but more often it seems to be fear of not doing well or assuming that the assigned task is impossible. There is often a lack of confidence that one's own utterance is a "link in the chain of communion" (Bakhtin 1986b, 76).

Jim and Carolyn

We also responded to the sentence rather than the utterance in the "dungeons and dragons" piece. In many ways, Jim was the most "roguish" student. He appeared to show absolute disregard for the assignment and for the conventions of academic discourse. Many of his sentences were not sentences at all, but fragments of one or two words. The sentences were confusing; meaning eluded us. Because Jim is shy, reticent and not easily engaged in dialogue, the context of this utterance was never clear.

There is always a context, however. Jim did finally explain that he had been afraid to try to write anything else. One of Jim's professors was able to talk with him and discovered that chronic illness which necessitated frequent hospitalizations for much of his life had forced Jim into isolation and long periods of inactivity where he had "a lot of time to think about things." The violence in his writing was often a result of his anger against institutions. Later, he returned to the writing center to work on a paper, and was able to talk with me about some of his personal experiences. These dialogues seemed to free Jim to some extent; in his more recent work, a connection, sometimes tenuous, to the class assignments has begun to emerge.

A Bakhtinian Reimagining of Jim's Story

According to Bakhtin, context always has primacy over text. Until someone was able to engage Jim in dialogue and support him in sharing that context, none of us could understand. Jim's "utterances" were far different from his confusing sentences on paper. When those utterances and their context became more understandable to us through dialogue, Jim was able to begin to risk and try to write more closely in response to assignments.

And yet, Jim's roguishness had something to teach us: something about him, but also something about pressures, about fears, about institutions. I'm not sure that we ever really had that dialogue.

Diane and Laura

Diane, who came to us with the assignment that asked her to respond to King's "Letter from a Birmingham Jail," had not done well in her humanities class the previous semester and was understandably anxious to do well in this course. She had been a reluctant and angry visitor to the writing center several times in the first semester after having been "sent" to us by her instructor.

Diane sat down and said that she did not understand racial issues at all; she had, she said, been raised in a small town where everyone "just got along." What would make people hate each other over the color of their skin, she wondered? In her town, "everyone just accepted everyone else." She had, in fact, grown up next door to an interracial family, a group of people she and the other members of her family "just accepted."

And yet she acknowledged that, while her family might tolerate her dating someone of a different race, her father would violently and unquestionably oppose an interracial marriage. She began to question the attitudes of herself and her family, wondering about their acceptance of the unconventional "family next door." As we mentioned earlier, though, none of the challenging issues and questions we talked about appeared in her final draft.

A Bakhtinian Reimagining of Diane's Story

There was so much tension between what Diane initially said and thought and the artifact she finally produced. I could have problematized for her the differences between the many voices she was invoking. I wanted to raise difficult issues for Diane, but she told me by her silence what she felt uncomfortable about. I wanted to be nice; I wanted to be polite; I wanted to help Diane do well in this course, and I wanted her to return to the writing center. However, by my lack of any real response, I did not allow any real dialogue to take place. Bakhtin tells us that "[U]nderstanding comes to fruition only in the response. Understanding and response are dialectically merged and mutually condition each other; one is impossible without the other" (in Volosinov 1986, 280).

Perhaps the result of my asking Diane these questions might have been a student who could begin to truly reflect on how racism operates in her world, who might begin to see how varying institutional agendas work to allow certain things to be thought about and said. We could have supported the "roguish" voices she allowed into our conversation, had we begun to investigate with her the consequences of allowing those disruptive voices into the academic community. Instead, I implicated myself in institutional silence.

Issues of personal responsibility as well as issues of gender, race, ethnic background, and culture affect all our interactions and our lives together. These issues are all brought into the college: dorm rooms, classrooms, our small office. Martin Luther King Jr. wrote "Letter from a Birmingham Jail" in the early 1960s. Our students were not alive when it was written, and King is no longer alive today. Bakhtin suggests that works that live beyond their own time are works that break through boundaries and live in what he refers to as "great time," gaining in significance (Speech 4). If King's letter has survived, gaining in significance, it should elicit a response. However, we often treat assigned texts as monologic; the writer has spoken, the words are fixed. We need to make room for and encourage the irreverent responses of the clown, fool and rogue if we want students to engage in "authentic discourse."

Knoblauch describes a literature classroom informed by dialogical rhetoric as one that, in terms of literature, "does not stop with 'personal connections' to literary texts but proceeds to a full awareness of the interpretive communities that shape those connections from the very beginning. . . . It hopes to make students persuasive by making them knowledgeable, to free them by revealing the means of living dialectically within academic institutions and the other worlds that those institutions serve" (188, 136). We like to imagine that the Bakhtinian notion of the dialogic nature of language might help us work toward a writing center similarly informed by these ideas. Bakhtin tells us that it is the very nature of the word to cross boundaries. He writes, "The word, directed toward an object, enters a dialogically agitated and tension-filled environment of alien words, value judgments and accents, weaves in and out of complex interrelationships, merges with some, recoils from others, intersects with a third group; and all this may crucially shape discourse, may leave a trace in all its semantic layers, may complicate its expression and influence its entire stylistic profile" (Discourse 276).

Our issue is not to "tell" students what to write, what they should or should not include in their papers. Our concern is rather that there are voices not being heard; there are contexts not being invoked; there are dialogues that are not happening. Can students truly make an informed, responsible choice about what to foreground or exclude from their papers if they are unaware of all the possible choices? Can we function as adequate responders to student texts if, for any reason, part of our response is silenced?

What Did We Learn? Jane and Laura

Jane, a first-semester student, had been a regular visitor to the writing center over the year. She told me that she felt that her visits to the writing center had been helpful; her writing and her grades were improving. Over the course of the semester, a relationship had begun to evolve between Jane and me, and she shared some information about her life and background. Jane, originally from a very small town upstate, found the larger and decidedly more urban environment of the college "disturbing" in some ways and perceived some of the people she passed on her short walk from the dormitory to the school building as "scary." Some of our conversations had centered around her adjustment to her new surroundings.

Jane came to the writing center one day with a draft of a paper for the first-year social science class in which she argued for capital punishment. The rising crime rate, she said, was due to light sentences for criminals and the "soft" living conditions in prisons that her father, a corrections officer in one of the state facilities, described to her. According to Jane, murderers should all be executed; she believed all executions should be a "surprise." Officers should just march into a condemned inmate's cell, Jane thought, tie his hands behind his back and inform him that this was to be his last morning on earth.

For the last ten years, I've taught in a college program at a correctional facility and feel committed to inmate rights and education. However, I did not volunteer this information to Jane. I did tell her, though—just to play "devil's advocate"—about statistical evidence and lack of correlation between capital punishment and crime and suggested she might need some "evidence," be it firsthand information or some other source, to explain to her reader the basis for her opinions. She vehemently resisted my suggestion.

"But it's just my opinion," she angrily exclaimed. "I'll just take that part out," she said and quickly crossed out that section of her paper.

When she left, I felt guilty and confused. Why hadn't I, a "believer" in Bakhtinian dialogics, had a dialogue with her? The conference was obviously tension-filled; I sensed many other voices and contexts behind Jane's utterance and knew I had not invoked the many voices sounding inside of me.

When Jane returned with a revised draft (minus the "surprise execution" section), I told her I had felt badly about our last conference and did not mean to deter her from any position she wanted to take; I saw my job as to help her articulate her position as fully as possible (something I had not, of course, done).

"You know," Jane said slowly, "my family is very racist . . . but I'm not. Because of where my father works, he sees a lot of things. . . ."

I still did not tell her that I teach in a prison.

Why? To be polite: because I was afraid she would be embarrassed by the position she had taken. I wanted her to return to the writing center.

I did not give Jane nearly enough credit.

I felt so uneasy.

Helen Ewald, in her article "Bakhtin and Composition Studies," writes that "I believe we have reached a point in composition studies when we can begin 'writing a story' of our specific and situational responses to ethical issues that arise when we engage in writing or the teaching of writing" (345). With the work of Bakhtin and Knoblauch, we have been able to frame a theoretical stance that allows us to "reread" or "reimagine" these stories. In these cases, not only did we fail to offer students any real support or assistance, we failed to invoke for them the full contexts of their utterances. By these failures, we perpetuated silence about the difficult issues raised in these stories.

Michael Holquist, in the introduction to *The Dialogic Imagination*, writes that there is "struggle and opposition at the heart of existence—keeping things together, coherent, keeping things apart" (1981, xviii). And, as we have already said, we suspect that this will be the condition of life in our writing center. Differences, necessary disruptions, and unexpected crises will keep occurring because language is living, not dead; it is an act, not a thing, an idea that lives at the heart of what Bakhtin and Knoblauch understand language to be. We hope that in the future we can be alive to these differences and disruptions.

Works Cited

Bakhtin, M. M. 1990. *Art and Answerability*. Ed. Michael Holquist and Vadim Liapunov. Trans. Vadim Liapunov. Austin: University of Texas Press.

Bakhtin, M. M. 1981. "Discourse in the Novel." In *The Dialogic Imagination*. Ed. Michael Holquist. Trans. Caryl Emerson and Michael Holquist. Austin: University of Texas Press.

———. 1986a. *Speech Genres and Other Late Essays*. Ed. Caryl Emerson and Michael Holquist. Trans. Vern W. McGee. Austin: University of Texas Press.

Ewald, Helen Rothschild. 1993. "Waiting for Answerability: Bakhtin and Composition Studies." *College Composition and Communication* 44.3 (October): 331–48.

Knoblauch, C. H. 1988. "Rhetorical Constructions: Dialogue and Commitment." *College English* 50.2 (February): 125–40.

Stewart, Susan. 1986. "Shouts on the Street: Bakhtin's Anti-Linguistics." In *Bakhtin: Essays and Dialogues on his Work*. Ed. Gary Saul Morson. Chicago: University of Chicago Press, 41–57.

Volosinov, V. N. 1986. *Marxism and the Philosophy of Language*. Trans. Ladislav Matejka and I. R. Titumik. Cambridge: Harvard University Press.

7 If You Have Ghosts

Michael Blitz
John Jay College, CUNY

C. Mark Hurlbert,
Indiana University of Pennsylvania

If you have ghosts, then you have everything
You can say anything you want
You can do anything you want
If you have ghosts, then you have everything

—Roky Erickson

In all of us, deep down, there seems to be something granite and unteachable. No one truly believes, despite the hysteria in the streets, that the world of tranquil certainties we were born into is about to be extinguished.

—J. M. Coetzee

Our stories—our own and those of the students with whom we have worked in writing centers—are from various quiet margins. We're not even sure that writing centers themselves are central to anything other than the living stories that fill, not only the students' writings, but also the air in the rooms.

"Gloria"[1] is one such story. In some ways, Gloria's is a ghost story. She came into the State University of New York at Albany writing center to work with Mark one winter in the early 1980s. He remembers the first day she arrived. *It was my turn to tutor. We went into an office to work on a paper she was writing. Like so much assigned academic writing, it seemed, at the time, inconsequential and is gone now from my memory. But Gloria is not.*

We sat down. I asked her a few questions to try to get to know her, to learn about the writer she was, as well as to begin to ascertain how I could help her—

standard practice. She told me she was from El Salvador and that she was in this country with her mother. She didn't say much else. So, we worked on developing and organizing her paper.

Gloria came back several times in the following weeks. We continued to work on the organization and development of her paper in these sessions, but she also always wanted me to help her with her English. Sometimes I would read parts of her paper out loud to her and she would make edits as I read, and we would talk about the reasons for these or she would read her own paper out loud to me and pause to make the edits herself. One afternoon, though, she stopped reading. She lowered her paper. She told a story. She and her mother had escaped El Salvador. Her brother was still there, and she feared for his life. She said that someone in her family had crossed the wrong man, and now her brother was in danger. She didn't know how he would get out. Then she told me about that national park, about the beautiful mountain—the view—the body dump. She asked me if I had heard about Puerta del Diablo. I hadn't. She shuddered, once, as she talked. I wondered if she was seeing it again.

Her brother, her mother, and she—all still in danger. She was afraid that her family—in America or not—was not out of harm's way. I wanted to ask Gloria questions, for more details, more insight, but something in her manner told me that that was not what she wanted. I also wanted her to feel safe enough to continue talking. I wanted her to know that I wanted to understand. But I feared that if I said the wrong word, she would stop her serious whispering— her careful explanation of the body dump and her brother. And quite honestly, I also feared what she might say next.

Gloria came into the writing center a couple more times, but she never talked about these things again—she only answered my questions about her brother to say, "We have not heard from him lately." Or about her mother, "She is well."

Then she stopped coming.

Where did Gloria go? We do not know. She came to the writing center to get her paper in order, to get her English checked, and to learn to write better. But we can at least speculate, now that it is fifteen years later and we have the benefit of Muriel Harris' research with ESL students, that Gloria may also have come to the writing center to discuss her problems with someone, to share and even to teach someone about her culture.

But why did she stop coming? Because that's what students do? Given the gravity of the things that Gloria told Mark, that feels like no answer at all. Perhaps Mark failed to say what Gloria was seeking to hear. Perhaps she could not say, precisely, what she needed from him. Perhaps, too, the writing center began to look as inconsequential as the paper she was writing for her class. Like so many of the students who are referred or find their way to the writing center, Gloria carried with her something more profound than a writing assignment, more profound than the problems with academic literacy that may have been one or more instructor's diagnosis of her writing. Gloria carried the stories which must be told and heard but which are easily lost against the "academic wallpaper of words" (Okawa 1997, 94), the empty formalities of what too often passes for serious academic work. The irony of Gloria's disappearance from the "center" is a deeply discouraging and potentially frightening one.

In "Negotiating Authority through One-to-One Collaboration in the Multicultural Writing Center" (1997), Susan Blalock reports on tutoring "Dan," a Vietnam vet who goes to her writing center in order to fit his military experience into a modal writing assignment. With Blalock's help, Dan is able to compare and contrast a memory of the Vietnam War with a visit to the Vietnam War Memorial in Washington. He even receives honorable mention for his work in a collegewide essay contest. But as we read Blalock's article, we cannot help but think that the assignment does not begin to do justice to the significance of this man's experiences. It does not call on the student to participate in and speak to a world in which war happens; instead, it is something the student writer needs help overcoming, getting done, past, completing. Of course, no writing assignment is as momentous as this student's experiences. But the prepackaged compare-and-contrast assignment, with its emphasis on formulaic thinking and writing, places experience and meaning second to the assignment itself. The result is that a tutor's efforts are often aimed at helping students to find some way to make a lived experience relevant for an assignment, rather than at working with students who are exploring and writing about life in critical ways. The result is that instead of being the place where students go to do serious, creative work, the kind of place that Katherine H. Adams and John L. Adams outline, the writing center takes up the default role of being the place where students go for some sort of compensatory experience, the place that cleans up after inadequate composition instruction.

In recent years, writing center and composition professionals such as Elizabeth Boquet, Lisa Ede, Nancy Grimm, Richard Leahy, Andrea Lunsford, Stephen M. North, Terrance Riley, and Nancy Welch have turned their attention toward a revisioning of writing centers, specifically arguing the value of moving our centers from places that reify institutional norms and cultural values to places that inquire into them. Writing centers can and should, we hear, do more than pretend to the central position (Leahy) or regulate educational experience (Grimm). They can be places where teachers and tutors examine writing instruction, the role of the center, the role of the tutor as teacher, the teacher as tutor, even how writing centers can be places for writers to discuss their writing seriously, rather than in "quickie fix-it chats" (North 1994, 16).

Who is important? Michael e-mailed Mark one night: *Quickly, I want to say, with you, "Everyone." But my experience—my real, everyday life at John Jay, in the heart of urban steam and sparks, tells me another story. Not everyone is important. Not everyone is safe. That's the lesson my students come to the college having heard again and again. Some have learned this lesson too well. Am I able to teach anyone—let alone everyone—that "everyone" is important? What about all the evidence to the contrary?*

There are things in our everyday lives, from which no one should ever consider themselves safe. "Anthony," a former student of Michael's, revised an essay under the guidance of his writing center tutor. The essay was a response to the direction: "Discuss an event in your life which you believe changed you dramatically." After the tutor had read Anthony's essay, he brought it to Michael, unsure of how he ought to respond. In a nutshell, Anthony's essay began with a description of his panic at discovering that he'd accidentally deleted an entire floppy disk's worth of writing—a semester's work for which he had no backup. This is a familiar tale of woe, and he was doing a good job of conveying that awful feeling in very dramatic terms. What Michael did not expect was the gut-wrenching analogy that followed in the essay. Anthony wrote about the murder of his little brother, who had been shot to death. Evidently, his brother had been hit by stray gunfire as he came home from school. Anthony compared the incomprehensible loss of his eight-year-old brother to the absolutely irreversible loss of hard work and creativity on his diskette. He said, of course, that it was much more terrible to lose a brother, but he also made the tragic point that such murders are, in effect, the same thing as pushing a "delete" button on the computer: one finger's pressure means irrevocable loss.

Anthony later told his tutor, "I probably shouldn't have written about that stuff." Evidently he did not believe, even after writing his essay, that the most dramatic event in his life was the right stuff of academic literacy. *When I finished reading the essay,* Michael remembers, *I couldn't say anything. The tutor nodded and said, "Yup, that's how I felt." In a way, we had no idea what would be the appropriate response to this story as a piece of required writing. What's appropriate? So many of my students tell shattering stories without a sign of a tear in their eyes. It's not that they don't grieve or feel. I guess, in some cases, they're just numb. Is it okay to say nothing? Is it enough to give students a safe place—a writing center, for instance— in which to tell stories? I ended up writing a note to Anthony, telling him that I'd seen his essay, that I was very moved, and that I needed a little guidance from him as to how I might best—or most usefully—respond.*

Gloria came to the writing center to fix her paper, but also for something more. She told about how things were, about what worried her, and maybe about a hope of relief. Anthony had been referred to the writing center because his paragraph structure needed fixing, but he was thinking about loss—his loss—all our loss. We surely don't suggest that one ought to overlook writing problems or withhold instruction; we do want to argue, however, the need for making our centers places for honoring our students' attempts at making their worlds more understandable, for creating ways of responding to these worlds, of being seen and heard when they are daily told in myriad, subtle, and not-so-subtle ways that they won't be.

In an e-mail to Mark, Michael wrote, *I really don't know why Gloria trusted you not only with her story, her fears, but also, later—right up to the minute—with the ghost of her presence in your daily thinking. I say this without a shred of authority, but I get the feeling that Gloria had a sense of how powerfully her words would affect you.*

Of course I know why someone should trust you—but I concur with you that there is a mystery at work, here. It's not so much that we are somehow "arrogant" in our position in relation to those we may tutor; it's that we are acutely aware of the arrogance we represent. Students do indeed come to the center to get their writing "fixed." (Don got the "The Fix" mentality of our age right in The Poetics of the Common Knowledge.*) They come for a weekly "fix"—a jolt of correctives to their works. A new set of works filled with the truth serum of literacy and academic propriety. We certainly do not typically fill the works with the moon and the wind.*

At John Jay, we have a wonderful writing center, staffed by excellent and sensitive tutors, supervised by a knowledgeable and caring director. Still, so many of our students consider a referral to the writing center as a sort of demotion. Not only do they have to do the work of an expository writing class, they must also now "report" to the center for extra help in a discipline they find uncomfortable to begin with. And so the initial hurdle for the tutor is to work through this "bad mood." Sometimes it's easy. Sometimes a student is so pleased to be able to pay close attention to her writing with a tutor equally devoted to the work, they hit their stride in the course of a few weeks. Others find the experience merely an extension of the difficulties of reading and writing college material.

Still others, such as Gloria and Anthony, find in the writing center a place of cautious refuge. A place to confess fears not only about literacy but about living and dying and running and hiding, about the loss of family members, of a way of life. Mark wrote, *I may have listened to Gloria's papers and so helped her to create discourse her professors could hear.*

But I administered no cures and no therapy. In fact, her Spanish-influenced English was beautifully eloquent. Her whisperings have been echoing through my thinking for a long time. The failure was not Gloria's. The failures are the killers and the oppressors and those too arrogant or lazy to learn the news.

Another story: "Allison" was in Michael's basic writing class a few years ago. *I'd suggested she go to the writing center when she did not pass her midterm practice (exit) exam. This exam is graded by a committee that cannot include the course instructor. Since Allison was frustrated and wanted as much additional help as she could get, I recommended her to Marsha, an excellent peer tutor. Evidently Allison told Marsha that she'd failed her exam because "a bunch of white men" had read the essay. When Marsha pointed out that I was also white, Allison told her no, I was a Hebrew, which meant that, while I was white on the outside, I was black on the inside.*

Marsha explained to Michael that she found she didn't know how to respond to Allison. She knew she could help with the grammar. She could offer sympathetic "sisterhood," as she said, regarding her pupil's anger about being judged by white men. But as she told Michael, "I don't know whether I'm supposed to become her friend, her tutor, or get involved in the race thing with her." We don't know, either. We don't know how one resolves Marsha's set of questions—and the writing center seems to be the place where these kinds of questions come up acutely and, perhaps, most frequently. Are tutors to be confessors? Friends? Co-conspirators in a revolution? Objective instructors? Lovers (as has happened in a couple of cases we know about)? Advisors?

Gloria may have left school to pursue paid work for a while. She and her mother may have had to move from their home into someplace more affordable or safer. They may have been deported. There are some who would argue that the best thing we can do as teachers is to bear witness to Gloria's efforts. We can point to her example: a student under tremendous duress struggling, nonetheless, to educate herself so that she can participate more fully in this society. But, we can imagine, some people will argue that none of this should be at issue; there is a job to be done, a process to improve upon. Blalock herself expresses initial discomfort at the personal nature of Dan's writing about his experiences in Vietnam: "As a teacher, I cringed at the prospect of a student's writing on such a topic since grading the assignment verges on judging the quality of the student's life rather than his writing" (90). But the stories are filled with accounts of suffering, with confusion and strain, with death and disappearance. This is, for us, the dominant "story from the center"—as told in these close-quartered, intensely personal moments with our students.

Gloria—

With me and not me
A ghost—a person a place
How do I tell this story?
What am I doing
For her for me for you
To her to me
If she is a ghost I can do anything I want
I can do anything I want
What brought her here?
How do I, with what I can, do anything to honor her
Her brother her mother
What she teaches
About living teaching
About the visibility of
Blood
Now, there is blood in my head
I can say anything I want
I can do anything I want
Except now I have ghosts
And I owe them everything
I owe them everything
Should I see bodies
should I see bodies piling up
And bodies piling up
The Bodies
Some raise a hand
Piling up
And some crawl off
A dump
Then we can do anything we want
And how do you turn it off
And how do you get
This snapshot developed
So it will never fade?

Gloria disappeared. But not completely. About five years ago Mark was teaching a selection from Joan Didion's *Salvador* at Indiana University of Pennsylvania. *Didion's description of the tourist postcards of Puerta del Diablo is chilling. I felt Gloria's "presence"—her effect on my life. I wanted to be true to this student's confidence in me—not because it is a burden, but rather out of responsibility. And here I was teaching a class of twenty-seven undergraduate students in a research writing course, most of whom had no more idea about the United States' role in El Salvador than I did when Gloria spoke with me, most of whom had never heard of Puerta del Diablo, most in a state of blissful ignorance as dense as the one Gloria had helped me with. I told them about Gloria. They were quiet as I spoke, and, I believe, shocked, and also respectful of the confidence I shared with them. They wanted to know, "What happened to her?" I wanted to be able to tell them. Their shock deepened when I told them I simply did not know what had become of Gloria nor of her mother or brother.*

In his book *Token Professionals and Master Critics*, James Sosnoski writes about "concurrence," the idea that we can enter into working relationships with students and each other that mirror "those among musicians who work together" (1994, 217). We think Sosnoski would see how important an alliance with Gloria is because he would see where it was leading. As he writes, one different teacher, one different course may not change a curriculum, a department, a college, a university . . . but two, three, four, . . . joining together? Can the writing center be the place for promoting innovation and affiliations among writers struggling to articulate stories and ideas that move them? Why not make the university a place for "centers" of all kinds? Seriously, let's chuck departments and divisions and set up large open spaces full of tables and chairs where people talk and listen and learn about things. This is the model for nursery school and kindergarten: a relaxed, stimulating environment, full of things to do, to read, to try out, or in the Reggio Emilia plan, to create long projects over. Just as the center itself typically does away with the walls that divide students into classrooms, let's "unfix" the fixtures.

In closing, we want to tell you about three people: two tutors, "Ericka" and "Leana," and "Sonya," a student. Ericka and Leana were two Rumanian women from, as they explained it, very different social classes. Ericka was from a higher class. Leana was from the working class, fun-loving, but also "coarse" and "raw" according to Ericka. Still, the two grudgingly became good friends and used to talk with Michael about how the writing center had become a sort of leveling arena for them in their teaching and in their understanding of their graduate work. As for Sonya, she was eloquent in her always emotional remarks about how the writing center had become like home for her. She was an African American who had been educated for most of her childhood in England but who had never been very good at reading and writing. She discovered that people assumed that her British accent meant she *was* really smart and upper crust, which she wasn't. She was smart, but she was not, according to her instructor, "fully literate" and was therefore referred to the writing center.

Her tutor was Leana, who had great success with her. But what was most moving was the day that Ericka came over to listen in on Leana and Sonya. Michael wrote: *I was in my office, directly across from the Center. I heard arguments and then laughter—lots of laughter. When I came in I found Ericka, Leana, and Sonya all laughing with tears in their eyes. Ericka and Leana had gotten into an argument over Leana's playful tutoring techniques, and then Leana, imitating Ericka's high and mighty tones, started answering her back in an English accent! This caught Sonya by surprise and then Ericka and Leana cracked up. When they explained to Sonya why the English accent had come to be associated with a certain know-it-all mentality, Sonya cracked up even more. She'd been considered a weak student in England, and hated the way she spoke and was trying to sound American. And what really cracked them all up was when she told Leana that she loved her (Rumanian) accent so much. Ericka had always kidded Leana about what a "peasant" sound her voice made and Leana had always admitted that she spoke, roughly, the equivalent of Rumanian cockney.*

The three of them were clearly a safe haven for one another in that moment, and that's what moved me so much. They had told each other important things; they'd laughed out loud not only in amusement but also as an act of caring; in some ways they'd gone beyond the expressed purposes of the writing center to discover at least something maybe each would only have whispered. If we have ghosts, they would be in the after-image of this scene and the occasional questioning voice that wonders why such moments of shared discovery are not at the very center of what we're supposed to be teaching, whether in the "center" or way out there, in those margins, where the whispers never die.

Note

1. The names of students and tutors have been changed for this article.

Works Cited

Adams, Katherine H., and John L. Adams. 1994. "The Creative Writing Workshop and the Writing Center." *Intersections: Theory and Practice in the Writing Center.* Eds. Joan A. Mullin and Ray Wallace. Urbana, IL: NCTE, 19–24.

Blalock, Susan. 1997. "Negotiating Authority through One-to-One Collaboration in the Multicultural Writing Center." In *Writing in Multicultural Settings*. Eds. Carol Severino, Juan C. Guerra, and Johnnella E. Butler. Vol. 5 of *Research and Scholarship in Composition*. New York: MLA, 79–93.

Boquet, Elizabeth H. 1995. "Writing Centers: History, Theory, and Implications." Ph.D. Diss., Indiana University of Pennsylvania.

Byrd, Don. 1994. *The Poetics of the Common Knowledge*. Albany, Suny Press.

Coetzee, J. M. 1980. *Waiting for the Barbarians*. New York: Penguin Books.

Didion, Joan. 1983. *Salvador*. New York: Simon and Schuster.

Ede, Lisa. 1996. "Writing Centers and the Politics of Location: A Response to Terrance Riley and Stephen M. North." *Writing Center Journal* 16.2 (Spring): 111–30.

Erickson, Roky. 1991 "If You Have Ghosts." *You're Gonna Miss Me: The Best of Roky Erickson*. Restless.

Grimm, Nancy. 1996. "The Regulatory Role of the Writing Center: Coming to Terms with a Loss of Innocence." *Writing Center Journal* 17.1 (Fall): 5–29.

Harris, Muriel. "Cultural Conflicts in the Writing Center: Expectations and Assumptions of ESL Students." In *Writing in Multicultural Settings*. Eds. Carol Severino, Juan C. Guerra, and Johnnella E. Butler. Vol. 5 of *Research and Scholarship in Composition*. New York: MLA, 220–23.

Leahy, Richard. 1992. "Of Writing Centers, Centeredness, and Centrism." *Writing Center Journal* 13.1 (Fall): 43–52.

Lunsford, Andrea. 1991. "Collaboration, Control, and the Idea of a Writing Center." *Writing Center Journal* 12.1 (Fall): 3–10.

North, Stephen M. 1994. "Revisiting 'The Idea of a Writing Center.'" *Writing Center Journal* 15.1 (Fall): 7–19.

Okawa, Gail Y. 1997. "Cross-Talk: Talking Cross-Difference." In *Writing in Multicultural Settings*. Eds. Carol Severino, Juan C. Guerra, and Johnnella E. Butler. Vol. 5 of *Research and Scholarship in Composition*. New York: MLA, 94–102.

"Reggio Emilia." Clearinghouse on Elementary and Early Childhood Education. http://ericps.ed.uiuc.edu/eece/reggio.html.

Riley, Terrance. 1994. "The Unpromising Future of Writing Centers." *Writing Center Journal* 15.1 (Fall): 20–34.

Severino, Carol, Juan C. Guerra, and Johnnella E. Butler, eds. 1997. *Writing in Multicultural Settings*. Vol. 5 of *Research and Scholarship in Composition*. Eds. Lil Brannon, Anne Ruggles Gere, Geneva Smitherman-Donaldson, John Trimbur, and Art Young. New York: MLA.

Sosnoski, James J. 1994. *Token Professionals and Master Critics: A Critique of Orthodoxy in Literary Studies*. Albany: SUNY Press.

Welch, Nancy. 1993. "From Silence to Noise: The Writing Center as Critical Exile." *Writing Center Journal* 14.1 (Fall): 3–15.

———. 1997. *Getting Restless: Rethinking Revision in Writing Instruction*. Cross-Currents: New Perspectives in Composition and Rhetoric. Ed. Charles I. Schuster. Portsmouth, NH: Boynton/Cook Heinemann.

8 Carnal Conferencing: Personal Computing and the Ideation of a Writing Center

Joseph Janangelo
Loyola University Chicago

Philosopher Langdon Winner writes that "as technologies are being built and put to use, significant alterations in patterns and human activity and human institutions are already taking place" (1986, 11). In this essay, I will describe one of those alterations and suggest that it signals a warning about the ways that computers can be used to foster exploitive interactions between writing center tutors and students. I will also trace my changing response to those events in order to show how such exploitation can reveal important connections between desire and pedagogy. Before telling this story, I wish to set the stage.

Context

The following events took place in the late 1980s at the writing center of a large urban university. Our B.C. (before computers) writing center had the standard amenities of an urban learning space—coffee pots, cubicles, posters, and rodents. It also had a popular nightclub underneath it. This meant that evening tutorials were often accompanied by synthesizers, drums, applause, and (sometimes) Buster Poindexter's live vocals. Then we purchased computers.

Our computers' arrival was a pretty boring affair. It involved opening boxes and moving monitors. Then things became glamorous. Our center was to have its "premiere"—replete with the guest appearances of English department professors and visits from the press. We were told that the event would be "special," which translated into the center being made clean. In short order, unsightly students and their papers were discarded, our carpeted walls and floors were steam-cleaned, and tutors were coached to say something optimistic about computers and writing instruction in case the press talked to us. In addition to cleanliness, the ambiance was further enhanced with trays of finger food and plants.

94

It may seem that plants are a typical design accessory for a writing center. Not at our school. For our institution, the proud recipient of an Erich Maria Remarque "special collection" and Paulette Goddard staircase, the word "plants" refers to the six to eight potted trees that were wheeled in to our public spaces whenever the press or VIPs like Jacqueline Onassis or Andy Warhol (it was the 1980s) paid a publicized visit. Before such visits, these plants were wheeled in from storage, unwrapped by their full-time mist-person, and arranged to create a green space within an urban setting. When the event was over, the plants were immediately rewrapped and wheeled away.

Skeptical of this coached optimism and temporarily upgraded ambiance, I was not surprised to read a contemporaneous *Writing Center Journal* article that described computers in an ominous way. The article's conclusion reads as follows:

> I have visited some writing centers of late. Some astonish me. They are plush, with luxurious carpets, modern (or post-modern) prints on the walls, secretaries, computer terminals, stocked libraries, spacious surroundings—and cubicles. I say watch out for cubicles. Watch out for computer terminals. Watch out for all evidence of attempts to break down the gathering of minds. (Summerfield 1988, 9)

Implicit in this warning is a fear that computers can contribute to the dehumanization of the center's mission and practice.

Two years later, while participating in Cynthia Selfe's wonderful summer workshop on "Integrating Computers and Composition," I discovered that the potentially dehumanizing effects of technology had caught the attention of forward-thinking composition scholars. Interpreting the role of computers in composition labs, Selfe writes that we often rely on "imported visions" (1987, 150) of what computers can and cannot do in literacy instruction. She argues that we tend to work within a "theoretical and pedagogical vacuum," and that our view of computer-assisted writing instruction is "circumscribed by the paradigms of other disciplines" (150).

Describing such labs, Selfe argues that, although they "provide the opportunity for teachers and students to gather together in one physical [location] where they can share information about writing and writing problems," they "are not guaranteed to encourage the formation of communities which share a common interest in written language" (149). Writing labs are, in fact, fraught with difficulties, including problems of access (some are not open evenings, making it difficult for working students and those with child care responsibilities to attend); problems of safe access for students and tutors; and problems of privacy (students who compose texts in public are vulnerable to visual eavesdropping). These spaces can also be constrained by their architectural design, with computers arranged in rows or against a wall, reflecting a machine-focused epistemology of office management, prison observation, and traditional teacher supervision.

Another compelling problem is the fact that these learning spaces are sometimes staffed by pedagogically untrained computer specialists who are more apt to give students "a technological comprehension" of what it means to write with computers, rather than a philosophical one (Freire and Macedo, 1987, 58). It is the complex interactions of one such lab assistant and one student writer that form the nucleus of my story.

Reciprocal Relations

I witnessed the following events as a graduate student tutor. One evening, while filling out instructor forms between shifts, I noticed that "Orlando" was working with a student named "Hedy." Because they were talking rather loudly I could hear that Orlando, who was sitting behind Hedy, was correcting her spelling (an unnecessary act given the computer's spellcheck program) and rewording her sentences. As Orlando's right hand covered Hedy's, the left one crept up her arm as in time to the words whispered in her ear. Orlando then brought the other hand up to her forearm and said that she could get "extra tutoring" when the lab closed.

My immediate reaction to this event was that Orlando was abusing the authority provided by the lab assistant role, as well as the body language permitted by teaching with computers, to sexually exploit a student who needed assistance.[1] Disgusted by what I deemed to be blatant harassment, I called Orlando into the hall, indicated that I knew what was going on, and warned that this exploitation of students had to stop. Orlando admitted propositioning Hedy, claiming that she "likes it that way," and added, "that's why she comes around on my shift." At this point, I said that I was going to alert our director, and volunteered to work with Hedy myself.

I then spoke to Hedy, apologizing for Orlando's actions and assuring her that such treatment would cease to occur. At this, she said, "Great, now who's going help me with the computer?" Hedy went on to say that she knew Orlando was "flirting" with her and that a "little touching" was "alright" as long as it helped her get "A's." Hedy also said that it was nice of me to "interfere"—that is the word she used—but that she could take care of herself.

What intrigues me about this "exploitation" is its intense mutuality. On the one hand, I saw a lab assistant exploiting superior knowledge of technology—something Selfe calls "technopower" (1988, 63)—and pedagogical authority in order to gain access to a student's body. On the other, I saw a student acting as a player in this interaction, using her body in order to profit from the assistant's knowledge of computers.

This mutuality reminds me of Foucault's distinction between "technologies of power" and "technologies of the self." Technologies of power are those "which determine the conduct of individuals and submit them to certain ends or domination." Technologies of the self are ones "which permit individuals to effect by their own means or with the help of others a certain number of operations on their own bodies and souls, thoughts, conduct, and way of being, so as to transform themselves in order to attain a certain state of happiness, purity, wisdom, perfection, or immortality" (1988, 18). Although the concepts of purity and immortality did not seem to be at direct issue here, I would suggest that, in reviewing Orlando and Hedy's interactions, one can detect a compelling point of contact between technologies of power and self, since both participants were using the computer as a tool of self-advancement and even abasement.

Foucault insists that the body is always caught up in such complicated relations. He asserts that

> the body is also directly involved in a political field; power relations have an immediate hold upon it; they invest it, mark it, train it, torture it, force it to carry out tasks, to perform ceremonies, to emit signs. This political investment of the body is bound up, in accordance with complex reciprocal relations . . . the body becomes a useful force only if it is both a productive body and a subjected body. (1977, 25–26)

In this case, the "political field" that the student's body was involved in was one of seemingly mutual exploitation. Orlando's implicit message, "I will show you how to use the computer and edit your work if you let me touch you," appeared to find a correlate in Hedy's unspoken response, "I might let you see me outside of the center so long as you help me use the computer and fix my paper." And the computer, far from being a neutral device, fueled this exchange by serving as both parties' technology of choice.

Theorizing vs. Venerating Technology

This story, on initial inspection, may appear to underscore the idea that writing centers and computers do not constitute a good fit and that computers are "highly threatening to a way of life we had carefully nurtured— a life that privileged human interaction" (Harris and Kinkead 1987, 1). Yet some writing center researchers find that computers can also be used to foster humane and equitable interactions. Consider Pamela Farrell's summary of her interviews with tutors and writers:

> [T]hey see the computer acting as a third party or neutral ground, encouraging collaboration, giving immediate feedback and ease of revision, inviting more writing, opening dialogue between writer and tutor, acting as a learning device, and giving writers pride in their work. If the computer does, in fact, interact with writer and tutor in these ways, what more could we as writing center directors want? (1987, 29)

While Farrell states that "The computer seems to act as a catalyst to open the dialogue necessary for an effective tutor-writer relationship" (32), she is also aware that any technology is subject to the desires of its users. Suggesting that computers seem to strengthen the interactions between students and tutors, she reports an increasing incidence of "the computer ploy" (32), in which a student pretends to lack technological knowledge in order to solicit a tutor's help with writing the paper. Farrell quotes one tutor's comment that students sometimes say that they want help underlining, "but before they do that they want to know what you think or how this reads, so they usually have another motive behind their question" (32).

In reconsidering Orlando's comments, it seems that some tutors may also have "another motive" behind offering assistance. Farrell quotes one student's admission that "he does 'weird things' at the computer, because 'it's very easy to get to know someone when you're working at the computer'" (32). Indeed, as Orlando and Hedy's interactions show, it is easy to "get to know" (or at least become physically close to) someone while writing with computers. Their exchange suggests that writing center directors should anticipate such exploitation when training tutors, and begin discussions about who is made powerful by the possession of technological knowledge and who is made vulnerable by its lack. Center directors and tutors should also be aware of the various currencies of exchange individuals will use in order to acquire it.

While I still believe that Orlando and Hedy were using technology exploitively, I have begun to wonder if erotics can inform pedagogy in less damaging ways. Given the distance of time, I have begun to wonder why erotics are automatically perceived as exploitive, and why educational institutions are officially represented as impersonal, de-eroticized spaces when we know they are not.[2] I also wonder why sexual attraction and seduction, which "are incessantly and locally produced and productive at every level of modern culture" (Sedgwick 1992, 279) are usually absent from writing center stories and scholarship.[3]

My first guess about the silence that surrounds writing center sexuality (I am referring to the tension and impulse, not to the activity) is that our culture trains us to distinguish absolutely—and I would add narrowly—between the pedagogic and the erotic. The popular image of a tutor who finds a student attractive is one of prurience and unprofessionalism; any tutor who acts on this attraction is automatically (and quite rightly) deemed a harasser. Conversely, a student, especially an undergraduate, who is attracted to a tutor is often portrayed as innocent and precocious. At any rate, such interest between students and tutors remains disparaged and, by consequence, unrepresented in writing center research.

Yet attraction occurs in our centers with and without the presence of computers. In fact, in speculating that a writing center may be a powerful, yet unarticulated pedagogic and erotic space for conference participants, I am reminded of two stories that I heard from other tutors in our center. The first involved Vivien, who narrated at a staff meeting the "sweet" advances made to her by a "client." The second involved Jorge's humorous summary of his rejection of an undergraduate's daily chocolate rose; "I told her, the judge will subtract your age from mine and send me to jail for the difference."

These remarks are not intended to be precious or salacious, but to show that a doctrinarian distinction between the pedagogic and erotic may be limiting, and to suggest that erotic impulses can fuel, animate, redirect, undermine, and even enhance writing conferences. This perspective leads me to articulate my second suspicion about why scholars are so restive when it comes to describing writing center sexuality. I submit that it is easier to portray student-teacher interactions through a lens of what I call "pristine pedagogy" than to depict them in their holistic complexity. In other words, if there is a pretense that issues of writer's block, ESL, and thesis support can occur apart from the personal, social, political, spiritual, and erotic dynamics that imbue any human interaction, a simpler, more focused—and less "contaminated"—pedagogical portrait can be painted.[4]

Yet I suspect that representing writing conferences in their messy, even sometimes degraded and exploitive, empirical reality would provide a more complicated and insightful portrait of the many intentions that can inform and animate tutorials. Here I envision the writing center in the way that Anne Ruggles Gere describes composition—as a *field*—"'a complex of forces'" and "a kind of charged space in which multiple 'sites' of interaction appear" (1993, 4). By discussing the multiple sites of interaction that converge within a conference, scholars could speculate on the dissonant, troubling aspects of each conversation. This could open an inquiry into whether sexually charged interaction between students and tutors can mean more than just hegemonic harassment or simple usuary, and to ask whether the erotic can inform the pedagogic in nonexploitive ways. Speculating in this way could lead to abandoning the fealty to representing the pristinely pedagogical and encourage the creation of a more holistic and vivid discourse that sees itself as enriched, rather than "tainted," by desire's traces.

My speculations, which may strike some readers as a recipe for moral and pedagogical degenerescence, are intended to serve as a warning against ethical and intellectual ossification. They follow Clark's assertion that for a writing center to enact instructional and epistemological flexibility, it should exhibit "a willingness to entertain multiple perspectives on critical issues, an ability to tolerate contradictions and contraries, in short, not to become so dogmatic, so fossilized, so sure that we know how to do it 'right' that we stop growing and developing" (1990, 82).

Langdon Winner, whose words introduced this chapter, also speaks of ongoing development. Declaring that "our instruments are institutions in the making" (54), he adds that "[M]any crucial choices about the forms and limits of our regimes of instrumentality must be enforced at the founding, at the genesis of each new technology. It is here that our best purposes must be heard" (58).

It is a bit late to invent the writing conference or the personal computer. Yet writing center practitioners can reinvent our recognition and appreciation of their site-specific best purposes. Perhaps those purposes are ones that recognize and nourish, rather than denigrate and stigmatize, the gamut of human impulses and intentions that motivate technology's use. Perhaps articulating a bolder, even more brazen, discourse about the personal dynamics that infuse tutorials would not transform the writing center into an eroticized space (because it already is one), but would arrest the repressive silence that encloses a very real phenomenon. A more candid discourse would help create a much-needed carnal, as well as theoretical and practical, knowledge of conferencing. This knowledge might help all involved in writing centers acknowledge the tacit (or at least potential) presence of the erotic in human interaction, and deepen the understanding of how that presence may undermine and animate tutorials with or without the "benefit" of technology.

Initially, I thought that this story would be about the effect of computers on writing centers. Now, I suspect that it is less about technology's renovation of tutorials than about human innovation with technology. Having seen the catalytic potential of the computer in Orlando's and Hedy's conference, I agree with the idea that "New technologies invariably change human lives" (Wahlstrom 1989, 177). I would also add that human beings can exert a powerful influence on technology either by using it against its primary purposes (as Orlando did) or by exploiting an alternative power base (as Hedy did) so that the computer's potential can be used for personal gain. My idea is that Orlando was using knowledge of the new technology to achieve an old end (a potential physical seduction), while Hedy may have been using an older technology (the lure of an after-hours meeting) to realize a new goal (the benefits of someone else's computer literacy). Beyond scenarios of blame and recrimination, it seems that both individuals were involved in a very adult play with power, with technology and, perhaps only incidentally, with each other.[5]

I also wonder if the temptation to issue absolute codes for ethical tutorial interactions underestimates the tenacious ability of human beings to become irrepressibly (and sometimes insidiously) inventive when it comes to using technology. This operative dialectic of work and play (of conferring and seducing) suggests that some students are already enacting an inventiveness, a curiosity, a purposeful playfulness, and a boldness in their interactions with technology and one another. Valuing, rather than stigmatizing, those interactions could help us better understand the dimensions of our work. Consider Andrea Herrmann's claim that "computers make new demands on teachers to make changes: to learn more, to create more collaborative classroom environments, to work harder, and to become more creative" (1989, 121–22). Having witnessed and questioned Orlando's and Hedy's interactions, I think that what Herrmann says of teachers is also true for students. Once people get hold of a powerful technology, or devise a clever strategy for harnessing its power, even the most sophisticated machine becomes subject to human design, desire, creativity, and control. If I can find one sustaining meaning in my story, it is that this text hopefully shows, in the ways that I witnessed, a student and tutor involved in the activity of being creative with computers. This text tries to represent what I think I saw—two individuals engaged in a indirectly articulated, yet mutually understood, underground activity of making trouble, making out, and, interestingly enough, making literacy.[6]

Notes

1. Examining the moves of solitary authors, Christina Haas observes that "the limitation in allowable bodily positions may explain anecdotal reports that

people become uncomfortable and stiff when working at computers" (1996, 131). It would be interesting to examine the range of allowable bodily positions that can occur when two (or more) people work with computers.

2. My thinking is influenced by Jane Gallop's edited collection, *Pedagogy: The Question of Impersonation* (1995). Gallop writes, "In marked contrast with the rosy 'eroticism' of all-female pedagogy, relations between male teachers and female students are sexualized as harassment" (81). Critiquing the "powerful prescriptive effect" of such "gendered descriptions" (87), Gallop argues for a recognition of the generative presence of the erotic within "the pedagogical relation" (85). In the same volume, Susan Miller makes a brave point about the "ethical frustration [that] has been translated into typed regulations against fraternizing with the Other." She writes that "we are willing to acknowledge that we want to talk about pedagogy and the personal as sites of a guilt that we often turn into compulsive talk, to voice-over unacknowledged desires for students we can never fully master, dominate, or love enough because they will, we know, outlive and rewrite us" (159).

3. Sedgwick, interestingly enough, is making this point in the context of a discussion of Michel Foucault's *History of Sexuality: An Introduction*. She argues that this book "enabled a newly productive discourse of sexuality by clarifying the extent to which modern sexuality is already produced through and indeed as discourse" (279).

4. This suspicion that devotion to the pristine breeds dogmatism and oversimplification is evident is Stephen North's suggestion that "a romantic idealization" of the writing center "presents its own kind of jeopardy" (1995, 9). It is also apparent in Angela Petit's belief that a tutor should not choose between the absolute discourses of "collaborative tutoring" and "current-traditional teaching" by "constructing yet another purified discourse" (119). Both scholars advocate transcendence of the absolute in terms of institutional and pedagogical self-conceptualization. These provocations herald a "generative indeterminacy" (Petit 1997, 114) which may make our centers more responsive to appreciating and examining the relations between pedagogy and desire.

5. I wonder if Orlando or Hedy used these ploys on other students or tutors. My only clue, *if* Orlando can be believed, is that Hedy knew what was going on, yet "regularly" sought out Orlando for help. This alleged "fact" could recast Hedy as less of a victim in, and more of a player of, this game. Orlando was, I suspect, quite "social" as a tutor.

6. I thank Lynn Briggs and Meg Woolbright for their helpful revision comments. I also thank Susan Miller and Yola Janangelo for their creativity and guidance.

Works Cited

Clark, Irene Lurkis. 1990. "Maintaining Chaos in the Writing Center: A Critical Perspective on Writing Center Dogma." *Writing Center Journal* 11.1 (Fall/Winter): 81–93.

Farrell, Pamela. 1987. "Writer, Peer Tutor, and Computer: A Unique Relationship." *Writing Center Journal* 8.1 (Fall/Winter): 29–33.

Foucault, Michel. 1977. *Discipline and Punish: The Birth of the Prison.* Trans. Alan Sheridan. New York: Vintage Books.

———. 1978. *The History of Sexuality: An Introduction.* Trans. Robert Hurley. New York: Pantheon.

———. 1988. "Technologies of the Self." In *Technologies of the Self: A Seminar with Michel Foucault.* Ed. Luther H. Martin, Huck Gutman, and Patrick H. Hutton. Amherst: University of Massachusetts Press, 16–49.

Freire, Paulo, and Donald Macedo. 1987. *Literacy: Reading the Word and the World.* South Hadley, MA: Bergin & Garvey.

Gallop, Jane. 1995. "The Teacher's Breasts." In *Pedagogy: The Question of Impersonation.* Ed. Jane Gallop. Bloomington: Indiana University Press, 79–89.

Gere, Anne Ruggles. 1993. Introduction. *Into the Field: Sites of Composition Studies.* Ed. Anne Ruggles Gere. New York: MLA, 1–6.

Haas, Christina. 1996. *Writing Technology: Studies on the Materiality of Literacy.* Mahwah, NJ: Lawrence Erlbaum.

Harris, Jeanette and Joyce Kinkead. 1987. "From the Editors." *Writing Center Journal.* 8.1: 1–2.

Hawisher, Gail E., and Cynthia L. Selfe, eds. 1989. *Critical Perspectives on Computers and Composition Instruction.* New York: Teachers College Press.

Herrmann, Andrea. 1989. "Computers in Public Schools: Are We Being Realistic?" In *Critical Perspectives on Computers and Composition Instruction.* Ed. Gail E. Hawisher and Cynthia L. Selfe. New Yorlk: Teachers College Press, 109–25.

Miller, Susan. 1995. "*In Loco Parentis* Addressing the Class." In *Pedagogy: The Question of Impersonation.* Ed. Jane Gallop. Bloomington: Indiana University Press, 155–64.

North, Stephen M. 1994. "Revisiting 'The Idea of a Writing Center.'" *Writing Center Journal.* 15.1 (Fall): 7–19.

Petit, Angela. 1997. "The Writing Center as 'Purified Space': Competing Discourses and the Dangers of Definition." *Writing Center Journal.* 17.2 (Spring): 111–22.

Sedgwick, Eve Kosofsky. 1992. "Gender Criticism." In *Redrawing the Boundaries: The Transformation of English and American Literary Studies.* Ed. Stephen Greenblatt and Giles Gunn. New York: MLA, 271–302.

Selfe, Cynthia L. 1987. "Creating a Computer Lab That Composition Teachers Can Live With." *Collegiate Microcomputer* 5.2 (May): 149–58.

———. 1988. "Computers in English Departments: The Rhetoric of Technopower." *ADE Bulletin* 90: 63–67.

Summerfield, Judith. 1988. "Writing Centers: A Long View." *Writing Center Journal* 8.2 (Spring/Summer): 3–9.

Wahlstrom, Billie J. 1989. "Desktop Publishing: Perspectives, Potentials, and Politics." In *Critical Perspectives on Computers and Composition Instruction.* Eds. Gail E. Hawisher and Cynthia L. Selfe. New York: Teachers College Press, 162–86.

Winner, Langdon. 1986. *The Whale and the Reactor: A Search for Limits in an Age of High Technology.* Chicago: University of Chicago Press.

9 Decentering Student-Centeredness: Rethinking Tutor Authority in Writing Centers

Catherine G. Latterell
Penn State Altoona

> As I began to live out and interpret the consequences of how discourses of "critical reflection," "empowerment," "student voice," and "dialogue" had influenced my conceptualization of the goals of the course and my ability to make sense of my experiences in the class, I found myself struggling against (struggling to unlearn) key assumptions and assertions of current literature on critical pedagogy, and straining to recognize, name, and come to grips with crucial issues of classroom practice that critical pedagogy can not or will not address.
>
> —Elizabeth Ellsworth
> "Why Doesn't This Feel Empowering?"

From the first time I read Elizabeth Ellsworth's article "Why Doesn't This Feel Empowering?" (1992) she struck a chord in me, evoking memories of students I have worked with in writing centers and foregrounding my own concerns with the writing center's language of empowerment and student voice. In her article, Ellsworth questions the underlying assumptions of key terms in liberatory pedagogy. She writes about her attempts to put into practice teaching strategies meant to empower her students (92). However, instead of watching students become empowered, Ellsworth found that putting this liberatory discourse into practice "led (her) to reproduce relations of domination" between herself and students (91). Reading her account of the shortcomings of this liberatory discourse led me to begin considering whether the writing center community's talk about student-centered tutoring faces similar implications.

This essay reflects a combination of influences that have caused me to decenter—or stop taking for granted—my understanding of what student-centered tutoring is. One influence was my yearlong work with a student named Carlos, and the other was my turning to the writings of feminist pedagogists who, like Ellsworth, have struggled to deal with gaps between the discourse of liberatory teaching and their own teaching practices. Their struggle with these gaps, in part, mirrors my own struggles to deal with disjunctures between my tutoring experiences with students like Carlos and the language of student-centeredness I heard in tutor meetings and read about in writing center publications. As a result of these influences, I decided to explore more carefully the writing center literature regarding our notions of authority and of being student-centered.

What does it mean for a tutor to be student-centered? Briefly, the central tenet of this philosophy is that students should be actively engaged and invested in their own learning. The role of a student-centered tutor is to act as an assistant or facilitator to students. Although differences exist among writing centers stemming from the particular histories and contexts that invests each writing center or writing lab with its own set of practices, this basic tenet is one of a few important similarities existing in writing center practice. For instance, many writing centers assume that most people learn better through social interaction and that writing centers ought to encourage students to become "practitioners" (Harris 1986, 28) and critical thinkers in their own right. Moreover, student-centered tutoring philosophies have played an important role not just for tutors but for the larger writing center community—helping this community define itself in relation to the typical classroom experiences of students who walk in our doors.

Importantly in this essay, it is in *how* the writing center community talks about accomplishing these goals that I locate my concerns, not in the overall goals themselves. Thus, this essay attempts to reveal some of the underlying, and limiting, assumptions of student-centered tutoring through the lenses offered, first, by my work with Carlos and, second, by the narratives of feminist pedagogy. It is my hope that both of these perspectives may provide the writing center community with productive insights into tutor-student relationships. Before discussing the pedagogical concerns and assumptions writing center educators and feminist teachers share, let me begin with the student who started me down this path of questioning or decentering the idea of student-centeredness in the writing center literature.

Tutoring Carlos

Before I encountered Ellsworth's story and those of other feminist pedagogists, there was Carlos. My own concerns with the language of student-centeredness in writing centers grew, in part, from my experience as Carlos's tutor. He helped me recognize cracks in my taken-for-granted assumptions about what good tutoring is. A Hispanic student from Chicago, Carlos faced many adjustments when he came to a small, isolated northern town to attend an engineering university whose population is overwhelmingly white, middle class, and male. More than a little soft-spoken, Carlos rarely spoke; instead he whispered, so I began whispering too. For three quarters we met once a week, and, amidst the writing center clamor of tutors and students talking and phones ringing, we whispered back and forth.

Carlos's silence and whispers, and the distance they presented, challenged my beliefs about the concept of dialogue as good tutoring. I had come to think of dialogue as a technique through which students learn to take charge of their learning. Tutor-student dialogues create an atmosphere in which students are equally (or even more) responsible for the learning that occurs. In this way, tutors act as facilitators, drawing out students' insights. Because of Carlos, my understanding of dialogue had to be reconstructed. Typically, our sessions began with him pulling out a draft of a paper, sometimes an assignment, and shoving it way out in front of him on the table. Then, slouched back in his chair or sometimes hunched over, chin in hands, he would sit, looking out the window. In a year of tutoring, Carlos rarely looked at me, only occasionally glancing sideways in my direction. His paper always managed to be out of our reach, positioned far across the table from us both. Every week I'd think, "Do I start with him or with this paper?" It was an odd question, I know. Students, not me, usually start by directing our sessions toward whatever issues or questions are uppermost in their minds, but almost everything about tutoring Carlos jogged me out of ordinary habits and assumptions.

It is difficult to capture in writing exactly how Carlos and I worked together, but let me try to describe a typical session. Often, I'd begin by asking him for a cue: I'd ask, "What do you want to work on today?" Pause. Under his breathe came the answer, "That," meaning the draft or assignment sheet sitting across from us on the table. "What is it?" I'd ask. Pause. With his gaze fixed on the floor or out the window, he'd mumble something. "What?" I'd say, leaning forward. Pause. This time a little louder, he'd say, "It's about rap music and censorship." "What do you think about it?" I'd ask. Pause. "I don't know." Pause. "I guess it's bad," he'd whisper. "The rap music is bad or censoring is bad?" I'd ask. Pause. Sighing, he'd say, "I guess they both are." "Why do you think so?" I'd ask. Longer pause. "I don't know. It's in the paper," he'd softly answer looking at the floor. So, we would pull the paper closer and read it (I often read it aloud to him). When his paper was near us, Carlos backed his chair away from the table, and his gaze wandered around the room. I learned over time that this didn't mean he wasn't listening as I read aloud. He seemed to need to put distance between himself and his papers. After reading, I'd frequently wait for him to speak first, not wanting to direct him. "Is it okay?" Carlos would likely ask me. "What do you think?" I would counter. Longer pause. "It needs work I guess." Pause. "That's what the teacher said." Pause. "She wants more personal stuff." Pause. "What I think." Here was a direction for us. "Okay, what do you think about rap music and censorship?" He glanced at me quickly and whispered, "I don't know." At this point, I'd pause, thinking what to make of that. Sometimes, I'd suggest he look back through the reading to see if he agreed or disagreed with one of the authors—a sideways way for him to start expressing a personal opinion. We'd come up with a list of some of the attitudes expressed in the readings, and the session would end with him hedging close to one of them. As he put the paper away, I'd ask, "Does this help you with this draft? Do you have ideas for where to add your opinion?" Standing up to leave, he'd look at me and whisper, "Yeah, I guess so."

In over a year of tutoring, Carlos and I rarely broke from this pattern. Was this good tutoring? As with all the students I tutored, I did not want to direct him. Rather, I consciously tried to focus on whatever Carlos wanted us to discuss. I wanted to maintain a student-centered approach that privileged his insights, his ability to learn to answer his own questions. In our sessions, I wanted to send him the message that his paper was his to improve—not mine. I wanted Carlos to feel empowered through our dialogue to develop his personal voice in his writing. However, all of these assumptions about good tutoring became as frail as a house of cards when week after week I sat next to him waiting, straining to hear his voice, and wondering about his detaching attitude. Carlos helped me recognize three related inconsistencies with these assumptions about being student-centered.

First, Carlos' actions helped me realize the extent to which student-center tutoring helps mask the fact that teachers have ultimate authority over the shape and content of students' writing. What Carlos knew all along, and what I slowly began to understand, is that the voice he needed to develop in his writing was not so much his own as it was his teacher's. In this way, he began to reconstruct my understanding of tutor-student dialogue and of being student-centered. The distance Carlos maintained went beyond the physical distances he kept with me and with his papers—whispering under his breath, rarely making eye contact, and remaining removed from his papers. There was also a distance in his writing. He never elaborated on the topic of any paper with personal examples or opinions. Even the fact that assignments called for his personal experiences and opinions never swayed him into offering them. He was uninterested in opening up in his writing or to me. As a result, he consistently made C's or lower in his writing classes. When I asked him about his opinions on various paper topics, Carlos gave me one of two responses: he'd pause, look at me, and either answer "I don't know" or tell me what his teacher wanted the class to say. Over and over, Carlos ignored or refused my attempts to encourage him to develop his personal voice or his ability to take charge of his learning. Politely and quietly, he'd change the subject back to the question of what the teacher wanted.

Second, Carlos's actions helped me realize the extent to which student-centered tutoring puts students in vulnerable positions by expecting them to open up about themselves. As a tutor, I had grown used to having an easy rapport with students in the writing center. Like other tutors, my sessions were begun, interrupted, and ended with the stuff of student's lives—their course loads, their new best friends, their homesickness. With Carlos, however, our sessions were stripped bare of that chatting. The few times we talked about his personal life he revealed a life filled with the painful struggles that came from growing up as the son of migrant farm workers who'd settled in a high crime area of urban Chicago. The realities of his home life and university experience didn't lend themselves to easy conversation. Everything about him marked him as different, and, rather than expose those differences, I think he chose silence. He kept his voice to himself, sharing only the softest tones with me and shading his writing with it in only the most general ways.

Third, Carlos helped me realize the extent to which student-centered tutoring assumes that tutors and students have a similar social and school knowledge base from which they can relate to each other. Carlos and I did not. We might have been enrolled in the same school (he as a first-year student and I as a graduate student), but our similarities seemed to end there. It was Carlos who showed me this with his silence and his careful distance. I never doubted that the Carlos I came to know in the writing center—whispering, detached, and silent—was only one very small part of his identity.

In the end, Carlos taught me that writing centers are places where we see how the politics of the academy shape students' educational experiences. Too often their experiences teach them that the cultures and literacies that have given them a sense of identity are not privileged by academic institutions. As his tutor, I wanted to be someone who could help Carlos bridge the gaps between his home literacies and those of the institution. In whispers we worked together, but like Belinda, the tutor Alice Gillam describes in "Writing Center Ecology: A Bakhtinian Perspective," I often felt at a loss, realizing that Carlos was "stripping [his] stories to the skeleton to please [his] instructors" (1991, 5). Given the pressure students feel to achieve (and in Carlos's case, to survive), I sometimes felt I had "no choice but to encourage [Carlos] to 'normalize' [his] voice so that [he] could be heard and found acceptable in the academy" (5). In the end, I felt emptied of some of my zeal for the language of "empowering students" and of "student-centeredness" that filled discussion during weekly tutors' meetings and normally buoyed me through the week. In a search for answers, I began exploring the *how* of student-centered tutoring in writing center literature. In other words, according to our own discourse, how is student-centered tutoring meant to be practiced?

How the Writing Center Community Addresses Authority in Student-Centered Tutoring

Writing center educators have often argued that student-centered practices provide students an alternative to the often unequal relationship of power maintained in many writing classrooms. In her retrospective of the growth and development of tutoring learning centers, Marian Arkin provides an illustrative articulation of the perspective many writing center people have regarding problems with traditional educational approaches:

> My suspicion is that emphasis on product—on how many things a student knows—is really a way of disempowering the learner, of increasing his or her dependence on authority, an authority empowered by tradition; it is, in sum, the power of a white, patriarchal, essentially reactionary establishment, an establishment that encourages everyone to come to the game and compete, but loads the cultural dice in its favor beforehand. (1990, 6)

In response to her concern, many writing center educators have maintained a philosophy that seeks to empower students, that values the languages and the ways of knowing students bring with them to the university. Writing center tutors and directors have claimed the role of student advocate. Because of their insights about students and about academic institutions, in recent years, writing centers have been acknowledged as "having an essential function of critiquing institutions and creating knowledge about writing" (Cooper 98). Moreover, Nancy Grimm has suggested that "writing centers have much to teach the [composition] profession about how difference is managed in the academy and about how students' subjectivities are constructed by educational discourse" (1992, 5). I believe many in the writing center community agree with Grimm that we have been changed by our interactions with students, and this is perhaps why student-centered philosophies have achieved a centrality in the writing center community as few other practices have.

It is because of its centrality and because writing centers offer the composition profession a critical view of itself that writing center educators need to reflect on how student-centered pedagogies have constructed our practices—how student-centered practices construct tutors' and students' roles. After all, pedagogy is never only a set of teaching or tutoring strategies to be judged on the basis of "what works." Rather, pedagogy, as a concept, enacts a set of assumptions that, as Lusted contends, "draws attention to the *process* through which knowledge is produced" (quoted in Gore 1993, 4). Thus, in writing center tutoring strategies lie implications for what does and does not count as knowledge and for what good tutoring is.

When reading through several essays that address what it means to be student-centered, one notices that these essays inevitably address the relations of power, as we in writing centers see them, between students and teachers and students and tutors. For instance, in "Non-Directive Tutoring Strategies," Kay Satre and Valerie Traub contend that "Our belief in non-directive intervention is largely based in our criticism of the current educational system which operates by virtue of unequal power relations between students and teachers" (1988, 5). In contrast, suggest Satre and Traub, the power in the relationship between students and tutors rests more in the needs and concerns of students. Satre and Traub's notions about student-centeredness or non-directiveness—in their emphasis on tutor's responsiveness to students and on students as active writers—embodies a common approach or language the writing center discourse projects regarding this pedagogy (Arkin and Shollar 1982; Meyer and Smith 1987; Severino; and Fletcher 1993). Being non-directive, they say, allows students to feel they are actually being listened to, and this makes students feel more attached to what they are trying to say. And, because, as Satre and Traub say, non-directive coaches do not pass judgment on students, emphasis can be shifted away from "apprehension of error and toward the development of meaning" (5).

The discourse's specific advice about student-centered tutoring is, therefore, often aimed at ensuring that students' needs control their tutoring sessions, and that they remain the primary agents of their writing. Jeff Brooks offers a list of tutoring strategies in his 1992 article

"Minimalist Tutoring: Making the Student Do All the Work." The strategies have been identified frequently over the years as basic student-centered or "minimalist" tutoring strategies (cf. Edwards 1983; Harris 1986; Ryan 1993; and Wilcox 1994). These strategies include "Sit beside the student, not across a desk"; Make sure the student is "physically closer to the paper than you are"; "[D]on't let yourself have a pencil in your hand"; and "Get the student to talk. . . . Ask questions—perhaps 'leading' questions—as often as possible" (1991, 3–4). These strategies are intended to demonstrate to students that they, not tutors, are the ones in charge of the paper (3). Brooks emphasizes this point by contending that "the student, not the tutor, should 'own' the paper and take full responsibility for it" (2).

The notion that students should be the primary agents, indeed "the only active agent[s]," Brooks says (4), in improving their writing is based in a desire to empower students. Satre and Traub speak of "handing power back to students" (5), and in "Posing Questions: The Student-Centered Tutorial Session" (1989), Patricia Fanning invokes the notion of empowerment by saying that tutors should "encourage students to discover and solve their own problems" (1). At the heart of these arguments lies a belief that the best learning environments are those in which students actively engage in the whole learning process. The desire to empower students is shared by many calling for change in the composition profession. Yet, as Marilyn Cooper pointed out in her 1993 keynote address to the Pacific Regional Writing Centers Conference, though many support these efforts, it has "turned out to be decidedly difficult to enact" (7).

I would argue that, much like conceptions of authority within liberatory pedagogy that face increasing examination, the previously mentioned outline of student-centered strategies reveals a view of authority as something one "owns" and/or "hands over" to others, and writing center educators ought to consider the implications such a view of authority holds for tutoring practices. The driving force behind enacting a student-centered pedagogy within writing centers has been to create learning environments in which students actively engage in their learning. However, the view of authority as something owned obstructs those original intentions, for, as writing center educators continue to talk about being student-centered as a process of *turning over* power or ownership to students, the question becomes: how liberating is this practice since, as the conferrers of authority, the writing tutor retains much control?

Decentering Definitions of Authority in Writing Center Discourse

There are two related notions of power embedded in the way writing center educators talk about being student-centered that I want to highlight, in order to demonstrate some of my concerns with them: The first is the notion of power as property, and the second is the zero-sum notion of power. First of all, when writing center discourse speaks of students as owning their writing or tutors giving authority to students, that discourse is viewing power as though it were property. Such an approach is misleading because it equates power with specific objects. In contrast, I believe power is better understood as a series of constantly shifting actions. Certainly objects can be invested with authority. However, it is through the actions of people (in this case, students and tutors) that objects or practices are invested with meaning. As Michel Foucault explains, "power must be analysed as something which circulates. . . . It is never localised here or there, never in anybody's hands, never appropriated as a commodity or piece of wealth" (1980, 98). For instance, power is not inherent in a pencil in a tutor's hand. Power, or the lack of it, is demonstrated in how that pencil is and is not used in given situations by both students and tutors. Consequently, practices or policies meant to enforce or sustain authority only do so in the actual actions of individuals. As Foucault writes,

> Power is employed and exercised through a net-like organisation. And not only do individuals circulate between its threads; they are always in the position of simultaneously undergoing and exercising this power. . . . In other words, individuals are the vehicles of power, not its points of application. (98)

Unfortunately, too often for the sake of defining policy, the writing center discourse oversimplifies how tutors and students relate to each other. For instance, in the discourse about student-centeredness, writing center educators are being discouraged from acknowledging the ways in which *both* tutors and students express authority as they relate to each other—authority that is varied, temporary, and overlapping at times.

By constructing writing center practice around a view of power as property, writing center educators are overlooking a number of points of tension that exist within student-centered pedagogies. Earlier I mentioned the points of tension that arose for me working with Carlos. Other writing center educators and feminist pedagogists like Ellsworth have developed their own as well. The first point of tension is that, because writing tutors are the ones who are choosing to turn power over to students, this "property" remains very much in the tutors' control. In "Reevaluation of the Question as a Teaching Tool" (1993), JoAnn B. Johnson illustrates this tension in her discussion of how using questions promotes the tutor's, not the student's, sense of control. She describes this as a problem of "needs location" (38). Johnson explains that "when the tutor composes a question for the student, it is based on the tutor's perception of need within the student; consequently, the attention of both student and tutor are focused on what the tutor chooses as need" (38–39). Hence, it is possible that, instead of student-centered strategies enabling students to actively engage in their learning, writing tutors may be maintaining students' positions as outsiders whose entrance into academic acceptance needs to be controlled. In this way, the notion of empowerment carries with it an agent of empowerment (someone or something doing the empowering) that has begun to be questioned by feminist pedagogists as reproducing old lines of hierarchy within the discourse of liberatory educational practices (cf. Gore 1993).

A second point of tension emerges as feminist pedagogists (among others) have questioned the notion of students' ownership of their writing. When one considers that teachers usually determine nearly all, if not all, of the parameters within which students produce writing, basing tutoring philosophies on the notion that students own their writing becomes problematic. Decisions about reading material, method of organization, audience, format, style, and page-length requirements are often already made for students by teachers. This understanding must cause us to question the extent to which it can be said that students *own* their texts—a point which, in my experience with Carlos, was made painfully clear. And, perhaps, this will lead writing center educators to consider Marilyn Cooper's suggestion in "Really Useful Knowledge" (1994) that writing tutors might best be able to help students achieve agency as writers

> by helping them understand how and the extent to which they are *not* owners of their texts; by helping them understand, in short, how various institutional forces impinge on how and what they write and how they can negotiate a place for their own goals and needs when faced with these forces. (8)

Thus, a second concern the discourse of student-centeredness raises is that speaking about student agency as tied to notions of ownership clouds over the reality that teachers, more so than students, control what students write.

A third point of tension emerges concerning the scholarship in composition studies that has begun questioning the assumption that students' writing improves as they gain control of their thought processes (cf. Miller 1991; Faigley 1994; and Cooper and Holzman 1989). As Lester Faigley has noted, in the last ten years much theoretical work in composition studies has "critiqued the central abstraction in current-traditional rhetoric and in many process-oriented approaches to teaching writing—the image of the writer as a discrete, coherent, stable self capable of rationally directing and rationally evaluating its own activities" (1994, 215). Through the influence of cultural studies, feminist theories, poststructuralism, and postmodernism, writing theorists have recognized that "knowledge is always situated" and that writers "articulate relations between a possible self and a possible reality (which includes possible others) in their prose, rather than a one real self and one real reality" (Brodkey 1994, 239). In light of this, writing center educators need to question whether or not student-centered pedagogies may be operating under a narrow idea of how people write. In "From Silence to Noise: The Writing Center as Critical Exile" 1993, Nancy Welch comments on this:

> My work in the writing center at a large public university has also introduced me to students who arrive at the center already aware, sometimes painfully so, that their meanings are contested and that their words are populated with competing, contradictory voices. . . . Even alone, these students write with and against a cacophony of voices, collaborating not with one person but with the Otherness of their words. (4)

In focusing on principles of writing instruction that assume people's inner selves are unified by a rational logic, writing centers educators may not be addressing the ways in which students write within a multiplicity of competing voices which are flavored by their ethnicity, gender, religious identity, class, and position in the academy.

The second view of power embedded in the way writing center educators talk about being student-centered is that power is a zero-sum concept. This concept holds that, if power is "given" to students in order to empower them, then tutors must "give up" their power. By representing tutoring practices in this way, the writing center discourse may not recognize the constant circulating of authority that we know happens when tutors work with students—how their needs and actions interact with the tutor's needs and actions as well as the needs and actions of the teacher. This representation also encourages us to think of tutors who exercise authority as always bad and students who exercise authority as always good—promoting a clear-cut view of tutoring that is out of step with many tutors' actual experiences of working with students. In a series of interviews of fellow writing tutors that I conducted for a pilot study regarding tutor-student interaction, one tutor named Dave expressed this point rather well. Dave answered my question "What has it been like working in the writing center?" by talking about the kind of control he has as a tutor (as compared to the kind of control he has a teacher). He acknowledged that it's "a different kind of control" and that he's "balancing directedness with nondirectedness all the time." Throughout the interview, Dave emphasized this balancing between "control" and "keying in on the student's needs," and there is an awareness of the ways in which tutors and students may be expressing authority to varying degrees simultaneously, which the literature on student-centered practices does not reflect.

Rethinking Student-Centered Tutoring: A Feminist Rearticulation of Authority

In the course of reflecting on my work with Carlos and the tensions revealed in my close reading of writing center literature on student-centeredness, I was also exploring the same questions about authority in the literature of feminist pedagogy. Strong similarities exist between the goals of feminist pedagogy and some of the basic premises of writing center practices. For example, feminist educating practices are generally characterized as being deeply concerned with increasing students' sense of agency, validating differences, challenging universal truths, and seeking to create social transformation in a world of shifting meanings. Moreover, of equal importance to me, feminist pedagogists have begun examining their own notions of authority in the student-centered language of their discourse, and they are moving to resolve tensions existing in the underlying assumptions of their practices.

Reviewing the literature of feminist pedagogy reveals a movement, over time, in how authority is viewed. In the past, many feminist pedagogists addressed authority or power as inevitably connected to patriarchal systems of control, and, therefore, bad. Thus, in order to distance themselves from imposing an authority they view as denying dialogue, feminist educators concentrated on developing nondirective teaching practices and on viewing educators as nurturing facilitators (cf. Quinn 1987; Frey 1987; Grumet 1988, 115; Schniedewind 1987; and Shrewsbury 1987). In response to this approach, however, a movement is growing within feminist pedagogy that has suggested these original approaches may need to be reconsidered (cf. Friedman 1985; Ellsworth 1992; and hooks 1994). The question in feminist pedagogy has become: by presenting ourselves as not having any authority, aren't we supporting the very assumptions (that women aren't capable of being figures of authority) that the feminist movement sought to oppose? Also, Madeleine

Grumet has argued that by continually denying one's authority in this way, educators lose their ability to speak from a position of greater insight. In taking this approach to authority, teachers and tutors risk "relinquish[ing] the power of pedagogy" (Grumet 1988, 115)—the capacity to share their knowledge of the world with students.

Growing discussion of this nature has led feminist pedagogists to develop educating practices that recognize the contradictory nature of power. (To cite a writing center example, as tutors we are simultaneously considered experts or "insiders" by students and novices or "outsiders" by faculty.) Moreover, they argue that these practices recognize that each of us as individuals constantly negotiates among many different identities or subjectivities as we seek to empower students.

As a result of this new movement, feminist pedagogists have begun developing another approach that moves away from traditional views of women (and writing tutors for that matter) in positions of authority. Though women have and do assert authority in the classroom, this authority often maintains forms of domination, silencing students under the disciplinary eyes of teachers (Walkerdine 1992, 19–20; Friedman 1985; Grumet).

However, rather than denying authority, argue these pedagogists, people who seek to enact a feminist pedagogy need to realize the need to women, and others to whom authority has been denied, to claim a different kind of authority. Feminist and civil rights activist bell hooks suggests that it is vital that this different kind of authority not be based in patriarchal concepts of power or stereotypical definitions of women. She writes, "The suggestion that women must obtain power before they can effectively resist sexism is rooted in the false assumption that women have no power" (1994, 90). Instead, she borrows from the work of Elizabeth Janeway to explain that one of the most important forms of power available to those who have been taught that demonstrating power is inappropriate (i.e., women, writing tutors, and students) is "the refusal to accept the definition of oneself that is put forward by the powerful" (quoted in hooks 90). Exercising "the power of disbelief" is a basic personal power that women from all races and classes and people like writing tutors and even our students need to understand as "an act of resistance and strength" (hooks 90–91).

Importantly, refusing the definition of reality students and tutors are expected to assume first requires students and tutors to be open to talking about their roles *as* constructs, and to make their relationship to each other and to the writing instructor explicit. Writing center educators and students need to be open not only to negotiation of these relationships but also tolerant of the contradictions and conflicts inherent in this kind of educational practice. Openness to this kind of questioning would also extend to examining students' relationships to their writing—perhaps causing us to question, as Marilyn Cooper suggests, the extent to which students have any say in what or how they write.

Moreover, rejecting the myth of students' ownership of their writing requires us to face students like Carlos steeled, not with the repressive rhetoric pervading much student-centered practice, but with the recognition that both of us—students and tutors—have a "plural personality," that we "operate in a pluralistic mode" (Anzaldúa 1987, 79). Anzaldúa's suggestion is that tutors acknowledge that we all negotiate among multiple identities as we navigate within the university's or college's demands. We need to make that balancing act part of the conversation between students and tutors. As Gloria Anzaldúa writes in *Borderlands/LaFrontera* (1987), in order to transcend dualistic thinking that maintains hierarchical relationships, we must develop "a consciousness of the Borderlands" (77) of the ways in which we experience and claim many identities, many cultures, and operate within and through these identities and cultures. "In attempting to work out a synthesis" of these many and often opposing powers, she writes, it is necessary for the self to create a new consciousness—a *mestiza* consciousness—from whose energy comes "continual creative motion that keeps breaking down . . . each new paradigm" (80):

> *Soy un amasamiento*, I am an act of kneading, of uniting and joining that not only has produced both a creature of darkness and a creature of light, but also a creature that questions the definitions of light and dark and give them new meanings. (81)

I acknowledge that this view of authority does not assume, as most traditional feminist models do, that people (especially women and people traditionally defined as Other) develop best in a nurturing and safe atmosphere. This view of authority requires a more up-front relationship between educators and students: one that recognizes that open questioning and negotiation have a tremendous transformative, and sometimes discomforting, effect. Yet we must see this, as bell hooks suggests, as "a constructive sign of growth" (1994, 103). Carlos's experience in the university was not nurturing after all; it was not a kind place to him. How many times have I wondered if our experience together might have been different if I had taken a less passive role? If, instead of avoiding our differences, we had openly addressed them? The end result may still have been the same, but I cannot help wondering. Certainly, he decentered my own understanding of what good tutoring is, and the struggle he provoked in me over my assumptions about being student-centered have led me from writing center work to feminist pedagogy and back again.

Conclusion

Writing centers balance on the boundaries between students and institutions: At the same time students' private worlds and the public world of the institution are coming into conflict, so are writing tutors' roles as collaborators who understand the epistemological value of a writer's personal experiences and their roles as savvy insiders who demystify the complexity of academic discourse for student writers. Tutoring Carlos changed how I think about tutoring forever, and my concern with the language of student-centeredness in writing center discourse led me to an exploration of feminist pedagogy's attempts to rearticulate notions of authority in order to provide an alternative perspective of the ways we talk about issues of authority.

What feminist pedagogy offers writing center educators is another conception of authority, one that might allow tutors to develop more active roles because it perceives educators and students as expressing authority that is varied, temporary, and mutually dependent on the other. It calls on tutors and students to question how their roles are defined and to open these up to negotiation, as well as to address the hidden but ever-present influence of students' writing instructors on their development as writers. It is the project of feminist pedagogy to create spaces where people, drawing on their lived experiences, can reflect on the social processes that have shaped them in order to critique these social processes. My hope is that writing centers, long dedicated to critique of the ways academic settings silence and subordinate students, may consider how the paths of these feminist teachers and writers may reflect and extend our own paths.

Works Cited

Anzaldúa, Gloria. 1987. *Borderlands/La Frontera: The New Mestiza*. San Francisco: Aunt Lute Books.

Arkin, Marian. 1990. "A Tutoring Retrospective." *Writing Lab Newsletter* 14 (June): 1–6, 15.

Arkin, Marian, and Barbara Shollar. 1982. *The Tutor Book*. New York: Longman.

Brodkey, Linda. 1994. "Making a Federal Case out of Difference: The Politics of Pedagogy, Publicity, and Postponement." In *Writing Theory and Critical Theory*. Vol. 3 of *Research and Scholarship in Composition*. Eds. John Clifford and John Schilb. New York: MLA, 236–61.

Brooks, Jeff. 1991. "Minimalist Tutoring: Making the Student Do All the Work." *Writing Lab Newsletter* 15 (February): 1–4.

Cooper, Marilyn M. 1994. "Really Useful Knowledge: A Cultural Studies Agenda for Writing Centers." *Writing Center Journal* 14.2 (Spring): 97–111.

Cooper, Marilyn M. and Michael Holzman. 1989. *Writing as Social Action.* Portsmouth, NH: Boynton/Cook.

Edwards, Suzanne. 1983. "Tutoring Your Tutors: How to Structure a Tutor-Training Workshop." *Writing Lab Newsletter* 7 (June): 7–9.

Ellsworth, Elizabeth. 1992. "Why Doesn't This Feel Empowering? Working through the Repressive Myths of Critical Pedagogy." *Harvard Educational Review* 59.3 (August 1989): 297–324. Reprinted in *Feminisms and Critical Pedagogy.* Eds. Carmen Luke and Jennifer Gore. New York: Routledge, 90–119.

Faigley, Lester. 1994. "Street Fights over the Impossibility of Theory: A Report of a Seminar." In *Writing Theory and Critical Theory.* Vol. 3 of *Research and Scholarship in Composition.* Eds. John Clifford and John Schilb. New York: MLA, 212–35.

———. 1992. *Fragments of Rationality: Postmodernity and the Subject of Composition.* Pittsburgh: University of Pittsburgh Press.

Fanning, Patricia. 1989. "Posing Questions: The Student-Centered Tutorial Session." *Writing Lab Newsletter* 14 (December): 1–2, 11.

Fletcher, David C. 1993. "On the Issue of Authority." In *Dynamics of the Writing Conference: Social and Cognitive Interaction.* Eds. Thomas Flynn and Mary King. Urbana, IL: NCTE, 41–50.

Foucault, Michel. 1980. "Two Lectures." In *Power/Knowledge: Selected Interviews and Other Writings 1972–1977.* Ed. Colin Gordon. Trans. Colin Gordon et al. New York: Pantheon Books, 78–108.

Frey, Olivia. 1987. "Equity and Peace in the New Writing Class." In *Teaching Writing: Pedagogy, Gender, and Equity.* Eds. Cynthia L. Caywood and Gillian R. Overing. Albany: SUNY Press, 93–106.

Friedman, Susan S. 1985. "Authority in the Feminist Classroom: A Contradiction in Terms?" In *Gendered Subjects: The Dynamics of Feminist Teaching.* Eds. Margo Culley and Catherine Portuges. Boston: Routledge & Kegan Paul 203–8.

Gillam, Alice M. 1991. "Writing Center Ecology: A Bakhtinian Perspective." *Writing Center Journal* 12 (Spring): 3–11.

Gore, Jennifer. 1993. *The Struggle for Pedagogies: Critical and Feminist Discourses as Regimes of Truth.* New York: Routledge.

Grimm, Nancy. 1992. "Contesting 'The Idea of a Writing Center': The Politics of Writing Center Research" *Writing Lab Newsletter* 16 (September): 5–7.

Grumet, Madeleine R. 1988. *Bitter Milk: Women and Teaching.* Amherst: University of Massachusetts Press.

Harris, Muriel. 1986. *Teaching One-to-One: The Writing Conference.* Urbana, IL: NCTE.

hooks, bell. 1994. *Teaching to Transgress: Education as the Practice of Freedom.* New York: Routledge.

———. 1984. *Feminist Theory from Margin to Center.* Boston: South End Press.

Johnson, JoAnn B. 1993. "Reevaluation of the Question as a Teaching Tool." In *Dynamics of the Writing Conference: Social and Cognitive Interaction.* Eds. Thomas Flynn and Mary King. Urban, IL: NCTE, 34–40.

Meyer, Emily, and Louise Z. Smith. 1987. *The Practical Tutor.* New York: Oxford University Press.

Miller, Susan. 1991, *Textual Carnivals: The Politics of Composition.* Carbondale: Southern Illinois University Press.

North, Stephen. 1984. "The Idea of a Writing Center." *College English* 46.5 (September): 433–46.

Quinn, Mary. 1987. "Teaching Digression as a Mode of Discovery: A Student-Centered Approach to the Discussion of Literature." In *Teaching Writing: Pedagogy, Gender, and Equity.* Eds. Cynthia L. Caywood and Gillian Overing. Albany: SUNY Press, 123–34.

Ryan, Leigh. 1993. *The Bedford Guide to Tutoring Writing.* Boston: St. Martin's Press.

Satre, Kay, and Valerie Traub. 1988. "Non-Directive Tutoring Strategies." *Writing Lab Newsletter* 12: 5–6.

Schniedewind, Nancy. 1987. "Teaching Feminist Process." *Women's Studies Quarterly XV* (Fall/Winter): 15–31.

Severino, Carol. 1992. "Rhetorically Analyzing Collaboration(s)." *Writing Center Journal* 13 (Fall): 53–64.

Shrewsbury, Carolyn, M. 1987. "What is Feminist Pedagogy?" *Women's Studies Quarterly XV* (Fall/Winter): 6–13.

Walkerdine, Valerie. 1992. "Progressive Pedagogy and Political Struggle." In *Feminism and Critical Pedagogy.* Eds. Carmen Luke and Jennifer Gore. New York: Routledge, 15–24.

Weiler, Kathleen. 1991. "Freire and a Feminist Pedagogy of Difference." *Harvard Educational Review* 61 (November): 449–74.

_____. 1988. *Women Teaching for Change: Gender, Class, and Power.* New York: Bergin and Garvey.

Welch, Nancy. 1993. "From Silence to Noise: The Writing Center as Critical Exile." *Writing Center Journal* 14.1 (Fall): 3–15.

Wilcox, Brad. 1994. "Conferencing Tips." *Writing Lab Newsletter* 18 (April): 13.

Index

Editors

Lynn Craigue Briggs is director of the Eastern Washington University Writers' Center, assistant professor of English, and associate director of the composition program at Eastern. She earned her Ph.D. in English education in 1991 from Syracuse University. She is interested in responding to writers and narrative, and especially in the intersection of those two topics.

Meg Woolbright is associate professor of English at Siena College in Loudonville, New York. She teaches the courses Introduction to Writing, Advanced Writing, and the Literature of the War in Vietnam.

Contributors

Michael Blitz is professor of English and chair of thematic studies at John Jay College of Criminal Justice of the City University of New York. His most recent book with C. Mark Hurlbert is *Letters for the Living: Teaching Writing in a Violent Age* (NCTE). For over ten years, Blitz and Hurlbert have collaborated on a number of articles, book chapters, an earlier book (*Composition and Resistance*), and other projects dealing with cultural studies, composition, and the politics of literacy and rhetoric. Blitz has also published four volumes of poetry, most recently *Suction Files*, and has collaborated with the anthropologist Louise Krasniewicz on several publications dealing with popular culture, new media, dreams, and Arnold Schwarzenegger.

Elizabeth H. Boquet is associate professor of English and director of the Writing Center at Fairfield University in Fairfield, Connecticut. She is currently an executive board member of both the Northeast Regional Writing Centers Association and the National Writing Centers Association. Her work has appeared in *College Composition and Communication* and in *Composition Studies*, as well as in the edited collection *Sharing Pedagogies: Students and Teachers Write about Dialogic Practices*.

Patricia A. Dunn is assistant professor of English at Illinois State University, where she teaches rhetoric, first-year and upper-level writing classes, and graduate courses in composition theory. Previously, she was associate professor of English at Utica College of Syracuse University, where she was director of the Writing Center. From 1991 to 1996, she chaired the interdisciplinary Committee on Writing at Utica College, which designed and implemented a writing program that includes portfolios and writing-intensive courses throughout the disciplines. She has published a number of articles and a book, *Learning Re-Abled: The Learning Disability Controversy and Composition Studies*. She is currently working on a second book, *Greater Expectations: Challenging Ways of Knowing in English/Writing Classes*.

C. Mark Hurlbert was a tutor in the writing center at the State University of New York at Albany in 1984–85. Currently, he teaches English at Indiana University of Pennsylvania. Mark has co-written (with Michael Blitz) *Letters for the Living: Teaching Writing in a Violent Age* (NCTE), co-edited (with Samuel Totten) *Social Issues in the*

127

English Classroom (NCTE), and co-edited (with Michael Blitz) *Composition and Resistance.* Mark has also written or co-written articles for *Works and Days, Pre/Text, Composition Studies, English Leadership Quarterly,* and *The Writing Instructor,* and articles for *Changing Classroom Practices* (NCTE), *Cultural Studies in the English Classroom, Practicing Theory* (NCTE), and *Sharing Pedagogies.*

Joseph Janangelo is associate professor of English at Loyola University Chicago, where he serves as the director of the Writing Programs. Joe has tutored and trained peer and graduate-student tutors at the Writing and Literacy Centers of Loyola, New York University, and the University of California, Los Angeles. Some of his essays have appeared in *College Composition and Communication, Computers and Composition, WPA: Writing Program Administration and The Writing Center Journal.* Having co-edited *Theoretical and Critical Perspectives on Teacher Change,* he also edited, with Kristine Hansen, *Resituating Writing: Constructing and Administering Writing Programs.*

Stephen Davenport Jukuri is currently working toward a Ph.D. in rhetoric and technical communication at Michigan Technological University. In his work, he seeks to intersect the areas of composition, rhetoric, critical theory, and cultural studies. He grew up in a small town ten miles north of the university, received his BS degree from MTU in 1989 (scientific and technical communication), and returned for graduate work in 1992 after having worked as a technical writer for a small management consulting firm in Indiana. His work in the writing center at MTU has included both coaching students and coordinating undergraduate coaches in their training and development. Thus far, his scholarly work, like his graduate studies, has been an ongoing attempt to intersect pedagogical experience with studies of language in social and cultural contexts, especially including the roles of power, discourse, and other social forces in political movements and social change. He would like to thank Diana George for her comments and encouragement with his essay when it began as a coursework paper under her direction. He is especially grateful to Nancy Grimm for her specific response to his suggestions on his writing, and also for her ability to maintain a highly collaborative and reflective atmosphere at the Michigan Tech Writing Center.

Catherine G. Latterell is assistant professor of English at Penn State Altoona. In 1996, she earned her doctorate in rhetoric and technical communication from the Department of Humanities at Michigan Technological University. Her research interests combine composition theory, cultural theory, and critical pedagogy to explore issues in writing program administration—particularly the impact of technology on teaching and administration.

Laura Rogers is a writing center and humanities instructor at the Albany College of Pharmacy, where she also works with faculty on writing-across-the-curriculum issues.

Carolyn A. Statler is a part-time faculty member at Albany College of Pharmacy, where she teaches in the humanities/social sciences department and shares responsibility for the Writing Center. She received her doctorate in humanistic studies from the University at Albany in 1996. Her most recent publication, "Emma Lazarus," in *Nineteenth Century Women Writers*, was edited by Denise Knight.

Janice M. Wolff is associate professor of English at Saginaw Valley State University, where she also directs the University Honors Program. She teaches undergraduate courses in freshman composition, upper-division writing, rhetorical theory, gender studies, and literature for general education. She has published articles in *Reader*, Michigan Tech's journal, and in *College Composition and Communication*. Dr. Wolff has continuing interests in "contact zone" theories, representations of teachers in film, and media studies. She was a Fulbright Scholar Winter semester 1999 at the University of Umea, Umea, Sweden, and has documented that trip in text and image. She is also part of the program Teachers in the Center, designed to integrate teachers into the Writing Center at Saginaw Valley State University.